Trade Softcover Edition ISBN 1-59929-033-2
10 9 8 7 6 5 4

The editors would like to dedicate this volume to our mom,
**Marguerite Fenner**

*Special thanks to* Gary Ruddell, Cortez Wells, Bud Plant, James Gurney, Bob Chapman, and Rick Berry for their continued support. And special thanks to Joe DeVito for sculpting the Spectrum Awards.

**Advisory Board:** Rick Berry, Brom, Mark Chiarello, Leo & Diane Dillon, Harlan Ellison, Iren Gallo, Bud Plant, Don Ivan Punchatz, Tim Underwood, Michael Whelan

Artists, art directors, and publishers interested in receiving entry information for the next Spectrum competition should send their name and address to: Spectrum Design, P.O. Box 4422, Overland Park, KS 66204 or visit the official website: **www.spectrumfantasticart.com**

Call For Entries posters (which contain complete rules, list of fees, and forms for participation) are mailed out in October each year.

Published by UNDERWOOD BOOKS, P.O. BOX 1919, NEVADA CITY, CA 95959
*Tim Underwood/Publisher* • www.underwoodbooks.com

# SPECTRUM 5

## The Best in Contemporary Fantastic Art

*edited by*

## Cathy Fenner & Arnie Fenner

UNDER
WOOD
BOOKS

**UNDERWOOD BOOKS**
Nevada City, CA

# EDITOR'S MESSAGE
## Cathy Fenner & Arnie Fenner

The fifth anniversary of the launch of *Spectrum* might be the appropriate occasion to look back along the path the series has traveled, to shake our heads ruefully at the mistakes that have been made, to reflect on the trends and changes in the amorphous world of fantastic art, and to take pride in the books' acceptance by readers and creatives alike. It would be nice to sit back and take the time to engage in a bit of reflection...

Unfortunately, we don't have the luxury.

*Spectrum* is a bullet train that's always threatening to leave the station without us. When one volume shoots down the rail (to the publisher, to the printer, to the distributor), planning has to begin on the next. And, as a series that's intended to keep abreast of an evolving field, it is understandable that *Spectrum* is always in a state of transition in order to better serve the artistic community it showcases. For good or bad, we're always trying to grow and improve at the same time we're addressing the needs of the market place, contending with internal changes, and battling with purposely obtuse critics who just can't understand why we don't do away with that silly jury and pick the "best of the year" ourselves, *because Joe Dokes really should have been in there you know.* Yeah.

Our intent from the beginning was to serve as a forum for the fantastic arts, to avoid the political infighting and genre prejudices that plague other similarly structured competitions, and to reach an appreciative audience who don't normally buy art annuals. We've consciously tried to avoid razzle-dazzle design with the series, making the art and artists the center of attention rather than the package presentation. We think we're getting there. Beyond that, there's not much to say other than...

Thank you. To the artists and publishers and readers and retailers who continue to support *Spectrum*.

And a special thanks to the *Spectrum 5* jury who tirelessly evaluated and selected the art you'll discover in the pages ahead from nearly 2000 works and helped establish, for another year, a definition for excellence for the fantastic arts.

Now if you'll excuse us, it's getting late and we've got a train to catch.

*directors*

Cathy Fenner    Arnie Fenner

*advisory board*

Rick Berry    Leo & Diane Dillon    Harlan Ellison    Bud Plant    Tim Underwood    Michael Whelan

# THE JURY

TERRY LEE
*artist*

JOE KUBERT
*artist/educator*

TOM DOLPHINS
*art director of* The Kansas City Star

JOHN ENGLISH
*artist*

JOSEPH DeVITO
*artist/sculptor*

DONATO GIANCOLA
*artist*

*photographs by Lainey Kopke*

# Grand Master Award

## JAMES E. BAMA

America of the 1960s can be described in any number of ways and defined by any number of events: it was the Age of Aquarius and a decade of lost innocence. Years of social unrest, free love, and political assassination. Confusing, exciting, disheartening, frightening. In many ways it was an age of heroes, a time of monsters and villains and intrigues and adventures.

While the country struggled with the divisiveness of Vietnam, the civil rights movement, women's lib, political corruption, gay pride, and disenfranchised youth, the larger-than-life characters from a more "simpler" era reemerged on the book stands to capture readers' imaginations and reassure them that there *were* simple answers to seemingly insurmountable problems. But to bring these pulp heroes effectively to life for a new generation required the unique skills of artistic magicians: Robert E. Howard's Conan benefited from the powerful visions of Frank Frazetta; Jim Steranko put G-8 and his Battle Aces back into the war-torn skies, and Richard Powers and the Dillons brought visual sophistication to the science fiction field.

But it was James Bama who blurred the boundaries between fantasy and reality with his breathtaking series of *Doc Savage* paintings for Bantam Books; Bama who made the implausible plausible. Bama who raised the standard for excellence in the field that subsequent generations of artists *still* strive to attain.

Born in 1926 in Manhattan's Washington Heights district, Bama's youth was marked by struggle and heartache. His mother, Selma, suffered a debilitating stroke when he was thirteen and his father, Ben, died of a heart attack the following year, leaving Jim and his older brother Howard to assume the family responsibilities. A gifted artist from the beginning and an avid admirer and collector of Hal Foster's *Tarzan* and Alex Raymond's *Flash Gordon* newspaper strips, he graduated from the High School of Music and Art in 1944. Though offered an apprenticeship to cartoonist Bob Oksner at King Features, Jim elected to enlist in the Army Air Corps. As he says, "It was a patriotic time." Upon his discharge he enrolled in the Art Students League and became a pupil of noted illustrator Frank J. Reilly, one of Dean Cornwell's proteges. "As soon as I got in with Reilly," Bama recalls, "I absorbed like a sponge and I was off and running. By the time I was 24, I was at the biggest studio in New York City doing big-time illustration."

His list of clients through the 1950s and '60s, both in advertising and publishing, reads like an artist's dream come true. He illustrated stories for *The Saturday Evening Post*, *Reader's Digest*, and *Argosy*, produced hundreds of covers for the premiere publishing houses, painted posters for numerous films (including *Heidi* and *Cool Hand Luke*), and created ads for Coca-Cola, Ford, and G.E. But its his sixty-two paintings for the *Doc Savage* series (and his box art for the Aurora line of Universal monster models) that have insured his lasting influence on and popularity among readers and artists alike.

Although Bama left the field of commercial illustration in 1972 to pursue a career as a fine artist (a path which has brought him even more fame, success, and financial reward), the impact of his genre work is still being felt. Prints of his *Doc Savage* covers produced by Graphitti Designs electrify new audiences: a documentary by Paul Jilbert beautifully chronicles the career of a monumental talent. Why? Why does work thirty years old continue to resonate, excite, and influence decade after decade? Perhaps Jim's observation answers the riddle: "I loved that stuff. I *still* love it. More than the art I'm doing now, in a way. It's my childhood. I enjoyed doing it, frankly. I wish I had done *The Shadow*, too. I did Doc Savage with conviction. I did him as a real person. Larger than life, but real. I was in the right place at the right time and I think I have a childhood fantasy memory about it that other people wouldn't have."

Adjectives don't do his work justice, superlatives seem inadequate. Better to simply mention the name "Bama" to a crowd in the know and watch the heads quietly nod in unison, an unspoken acknowledgement of one of the brightest and best.

*b o r n   1 9 2 6*

# SPECTRUM

## THE YEAR IN REVIEW BY ARNIE FENNER

There's an old saying: "You can't know where you're going if you don't know where you've been."

So in examining the previous year's events, observers might come to the conclusion that the foreseeable future for fantastic art (and illustration in general) appears to be a little discouraging. The new proverb might be: "We don't like where we are and we aren't thrilled with where we're going."

Throughout 1997 many artists were faced with a devaluation of their skills and stiff competition for commissions. Certainly, there were those creatives who were constantly in demand and could dictate terms and fees, but there was a growing segment of the community that had to contend with a "buyer's market" mentality among clients. Prices were down, jobs were fewer, and illustrators found themselves competing with graphic designers and computer artists in a genre that had until recently rarely acknowledged the existence of either art form.

The issue of digitally-available stock illustration (the practice of selling rights to previously published works, usually through a third-party company) became a topic of hot debate in various artist associations: advocates were obviously happy with the additional income while opponents complained about declining original commissions and an open invitation to purchasers to alter another's art. Their position was buttressed near the end of the year by an incident in which five separate publishers, unbeknownst to each other, purchased and used the same digital artwork by Eric Dinyer from a stock company on five markedly different books.

The implications of the digital revolution and its effects on the arts are numerous and far reaching and seem to mutate almost daily with the introduction of new equipment, software, and client sensibilities. Companies are able to scan and utilize artists' works without acknowledging copyrights until they're caught (if they ever are). Clients routinely demand changes in digital art that would have been unthinkable with work created in traditional mediums—not necessarily to improve the art in question, but rather because of the perception that digital images can be manipulated and revised with seeming ease, so, why not? The Internet, with its world-wide web of anonymous users, has become conversely a wonderful (if over-hyped) research, communication, and marketing tool while simultaneously serving as the single largest vehicle for

*Oh, my God! They killed Kenney! Those bastards! Featuring alien abductions, MechaStreisand monsters, and science experiments gone horribly wrong, Trey Parker's and Matt Stone's hilariously irreverent animated* South Park *on cable TV's Comedy Central became* the *hot show of 1997. By year's end a variety of spin-off products began to appear, but no Mr. Hanky (The Christmas Poo) action figure. It's probably only a matter of time.* Copyright © 1998 by Comedy Central.

outrageously blatant copyright infringement by every hotdog with a flatbed scanner. And despite the rampant health problems directly connected to increased computer usage, the courts and employers wink at each other and deny liability for their workers' carpal tunnel and repetitive stress injuries. Just do the work and stop whining!

But love it or loathe it, the computer in one form or another is here to stay: savvy artists in every medium will need to be aware of its uses if they wish to stay competitive in an evolving market. Not to say that anyone should throw away their paints or sculpy and start shopping for a Mac G3. Regardless of the sophistication or finesse of a computer image, there is still nothing that intrigues the eye, nothing that "feels" like an original oil or bronze. But to deny that the digital world is rapidly impacting on the traditional art world, that it offers a wealth of possibilities to illustrators and painters (if, for nothing else,

inexpensively archiving their work), is a folly that ultimately could spell disaster. Typesetters laughed at the prospect of individuals generating their own professional type fifteen years ago. Then came PageMaker and Quark Express and Illustrator and Freehand.

Who's laughing now?

Gloomy thoughts? Not really. Simply some observations about the evolution of the form. There are always areas for concern, just as there are reasons to celebrate. Evolution is a part of the natural process, and in 1997 it was obvious that although things maybe weren't quite as comfortable as they'd been in the past, the fantastic arts were alive and kicking.

## ADVERTISING

It's not easy to keep track of credits in the world of advertising: there are campaigns and strategies that differ radically from market to market, regional promotions geared specifically to local demographics, and direct mail promotions that are impossible to chart. And as only one of the many gears in the advertising machinery it is rare that the artist receives any credit for their work—the product is what is meant to get your attention, not the creatives that attracted you to it.

And as I've said in previous volumes of *Spectrum*, the computer (and particularly Photoshop) has had a profound effect on the fast-paced world of advertising. No longer reliant on prohibitively priced set constructions and photo shoots or on illustrators with conflicting schedules, agencies regularly achieve elaborate fantastic set-ups by combining and manipulating stock photos and graphics. Virtually every movie poster and promotion utilizes digital imagery—the glory days of Bob Peak or Frank McCarthy film art are quickly becoming nostalgic memories. Undoubtedly, the cycle will eventually bring illustration back into vogue in the future, but for now computer-enhanced photography rules the ad roost.

Of the art I've seen over the past year that I was especially impressed with (and was able to find credits for—never easy in print advertising) Mark Summers' pen and ink genie for the Yale-New Haven Health system, Gary Kelley's promotional poster for *Morality Play* [client: W.W. Norton], Daniel Craig's *Brigadoon* poster for the New York City Opera, René Milot's painting for *The Turn of the Screw* for the same client, and any number of Rafal Olbinski's wonderfully Magritte-flavored theater posters. There are numerous regional and national trade publications for the advertising industry, but excellent resources for those interested in keeping abreast of the latest trends are *Print*, *Communication Arts*, and *Step-By-Step Graphics*—all available at larger bookstores and newsstands.

## EDITORIAL

There was a time (not so terribly long ago) when the parameters of the fantasy and science fiction field were determined by the genre magazines. Of course, that was pre-*Star Wars*, pre-mass-media, and definitely pre-WWW.com.

After *Omni*'s departure for cyberspace several years ago, it was feared that the genre fiction magazines would tumble into oblivion like so many dominoes, leaving only those titles that catered to film/TV or gaming audiences. Since modern SF is firmly rooted in short fiction there has always been the fear that a failure of the magazines would spell disaster for the field as a whole

Yet, despite declining circulations and an aging reader demographic the various fiction titles held on throughout '97—many predicted a healthier 1998—and there was a normal influx of new (albeit short-lived) titles.

Sovereign Media's *Science Fiction Age* and *Realms of Fantasy* were the flashiest genre titles on the racks. Though reliant on reprint covers and rather conservative in layout and illustrative preferences, the magazines nevertheless featured some affecting full color art by Steven Adler, John Berkey, and John K. Snyder III, along with welcome profiles of often overlooked masters like Manuel Sanjulian and Richard Bober.

The less-flashy f&sf digest-sized magazines were, if anything, consistent in quality. *Analog* and *Asimov's Science Fiction Magazine* featured indifferently executed interior drawings, but compensated with a nice selection of cover paintings by George Krauter, Barclay Shaw, and Bob Eggleton. *The Magazine of Fantasy & Science Fiction*, ever the sophisticate among the surviving pulps, published some wonderful covers by Ron Walotsky, Mark Rich, and Barclay Shaw.

The smaller genre magazines, with their tight budgets and amateur art direction,

served more as a proving ground than a showcase for many new and part-time illustrators. Titles like *Cemetery Dance*, England's *Interzone, Eiodelin*, and *Marion Zimmer Bradley's Fantasy Magazine* (which included an exceptional cover by professional painter Nicolas Jainschigg) are similar in many ways to the better fanzines of the 1960s and '70s (like Tom Reamy's influential *Trumpet*, Richard Geis' *Science Fiction Review*, or George Scithers' *Amra*): they're a great place to watch for emerging artistic talent.

Fantastic art naturally cropped up on a regular basis within non-genre magazines. I am constantly amazed and impressed with the

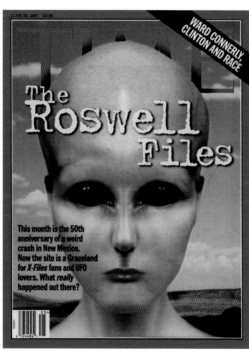

WARD CONNERLY CLINTON AND RACE

*The 50th anniversary of the saucer "crash" at Roswell, New Mexico, prompted stories in virtually every media and market. Matt Mahurin's cover for* Time *was only one of many illustrations that celebrated society's growing fascination with alien proctologists.*

scope, quality and quantity of excellent work published each year in *Playboy*. Art directed by Tom Staebler, it remains the single largest and classiest forum for narrative illustration being published today: they have performed an amazing balancing act of embracing the cutting edge while never sacrificing clarity. Pictures of nekkid ladies obscures the fact for some critics that *Playboy* is pretty much the only surviving link to the mythic Golden Age of editorial art: work by Tim O'Brian, Kinuko Y. Craft, Marshall Arisman, Mel Odom, and Donato Giancola published throughout their pages in 1997 once again proved the point.

*Mad*, the perennial naughty boy of humor magazines, went through some changes last year with an influx of new artists and a rougher comic attitude that became a source

of some controversy. Though several of it's legendary creators elected to bow out of the line-up, *Mad* was still a marvelous treasure-trove of exceptional talent, publishing work by Angelo Torres, Sergio Arogonnes, Mort Drucker, Tom Bunk, Peter Kuper, and Joe Devito.

*Outré* expanded its pop-culture horizons with articles about artists Chesley Bonestall and Vincent DiFate along with a fascinating ongoing funny and tragic biography of comic book genius Wallace Wood. And, the 50th anniversary of the "alien crash" at Roswell, New Mexico, had every magazine from *Time* to *Disney Adventures* hopping on the extraterrestrial band-wagon with coverage and tons of appropriate illustrations.

Certainly, memorable art was readily apparent in magazines as diverse as *The New Yorker, Boy's Life, Rolling Stone* (which published some outstanding work by Anita Kuntz and C.F. Payne), and *Texas Monthly* for those who kept their eyes open.

Although there is no single publication that keeps track of the infinite venues for the fantastic arts, one reliable and interesting starting point is *Locus*, the monthly trade journal for the science fiction and fantasy genres.($5.00 for a sample copy to Locus Publications, P.O. Box 5545, Oakland, CA 95945.)

## BOOKS

If anything was obvious in the book world last year (and damned few things were) it was that graphic designers were dominating a market that until recently had been the illustrators' private territory. Typography, manipulated photographs, clip art, and simple spot motifs were much more prevalent on covers than were narrative paintings. Indeed, Avon made a point of announcing that their relaunched science fiction line would feature flat-graphic jackets instead of traditional cover art.

Of course, graphic book jackets aren't anything new—just look at any brand-name bestseller—but it *is* something of a departure for the fantasy and science fiction field, whose readers have tended to be more appreciative of genre painters. The use of classic fine art works and stock imagery was more obvious than ever, undoubtedly as a result of budget constraints rather than as an attempt by the art directors to make an aesthetic statement. There were fewer books from the more reliable small presses, several publishers filed for bankruptcy, and others (like Turner) were absorbed and discontinued in mergers with larger corporations.

*The New Yorker* published an interesting

article about the book industry and stated quite matter-of-factly that there *always* seems to be the perception within the industry of some sort of crisis in publishing: blame has to be assigned, penance must be paid, changes

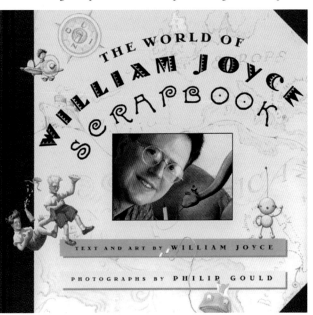

The World of William Joyce Scrapbook *was a wonderful overview of the career of one of today's finest (and funniest) children's book creators.*

have to be made in order to keep the sky from falling. And it appears that presently it's the art departments (and, more importantly, their budgets) that are having to answer for the alarmed cries of the editorial Henny Pennys. (Though book sales, at least in dollar figures, are actually at an all-time high.) Time and returns of unsold books will tell whether this is a short-cycled fad or a long-term trend in publishing. Hopefully it will be the former rather than the latter.

Still, a quick glance at the bookshelves (or at the website of your favorite on-line bookseller) made it obvious that there was still a wondrous variety of terrific art that saw print in 1997.

Donato Giancola has quickly established himself as one of the hottest new stars of narrative genre art. Certainly not limited to a single subject or perspective, his covers for *Fool's War* by Sarah Zettel (Warner) and *Dry Water* by Eric Nylund (Avon) showcased a combination of technical savvy with a keen dramatic flair.

John Jude Palencar's cool and sophisticated covers for *Desperation* by Stephen King, *The Regulators* by "Richard Bachman," (both for Penguin) and *Archangel* by Sharon Shin (Ace) were prime examples of fine art brilliantly applied to a commercial product. Greg Spalinka's painting for *Jack Faust* by Michael Swanwick (Avon) was equally successful.

Gregory Bridges's cover for *An exchange of Hostages* (by Susan Matthews, AvoNova),

Cliff Nielson's for *The Crow: Quoth the Crow* (by David Bischoff, HarperPrism), and Keith Birdsong's painting for the anthology *The Magic Lover's Treasury of the Fantastic* (Warner/Aspect) were all disparate in techniques and all cheerfully embraced the genre with gusto.

Other covers worth noting include those by Tim O'Brian (*The Illustrated Man* by Ray Bradbury [Avon]), Vincent DiFate (*The Billion Dollar Boy* by Charles Sheffield [Tor]), Rick Berry (*Sailing to Utopia* by Michael Moorcock [Whitewolf]), Grand Masters Leo and Diane Dillon (*Sabriel* by Garth Nix [HarperCollins]), Mary Grand Pré (*In the Land of Winter* by Richard Grant [Avon]), Gary Ruddell (*The Rise of Endymion* by Dan Simmons [Bantam]), Tom Canty (*The Year's Best Fantasy & Horror Vol. X* edited by Terri Windling and Ellen Datlow [St. Martin's]), Eric Rohmann (*His Dark Materials 2* by Phillip Pullman [Bantam]), and Doug Beekman (*Dune* by Frank Herbert [Eastman Press]). This most definitely is not a comprehensive list of all of the exemplary covers produced last year (nor is it meant to be), but merely some that have stuck in my memory.

There was a welcome stack of beautifully illustrated volumes for both adults and children released in '97—perhaps for obvious reasons fantasy and SF seem to be the last bastions for illustrated fiction and that fact is not lost on many gifted creators.

Alan Lee's paintings for the 60th anniversary edition of J.R.R. Tolkien's *The Hobbit* (Houghton Miflin) reinforced his reputation as one of the finest fantasy artists of the latter 20th century. The mystical quality of his work seems especially well suited to Tolkien's epic. Rick Berry wowed readers with his interpretation of Harlan Ellison's *"Repent, Harlequin!" Said the Ticktockman* (Underwood Books), James C. Christensen charmingly wrote and illustrated *Rhymes & Reasons* (Greenwich Workshop/Artisan), and Paul O. Zelinsky wonderfully re-adapted *Rapunzel* (Dutton). Film director Tim Burton gave a rare glimpse of his drawing abilities with his fiction collection *The Melancholy Death of Oyster Boy and Other Stories* (Weisbach/Morrow), Barry Moser's work enhanced Virginia Hamilton's *A Ring of Tricksters* (Bluesky/Scho-

lastic), and John Howe thoroughly explored *A Diversity of Dragons* by Anne McCaffrey (Harper Prism).

Other illustrated volumes worth scoping out included *The Cinder-Eyed Cats* (written and illustrated by Eric Rohmann [Crown]), *Nicholas Pipe* by Robert D. SanSouci (paintings by the always wonderful David Shannon [Dial]), *The Great Kettles: A Tale of Time* (story and art by *The Ship of Dream*'s Dean Morrissey [Abrams]), *Hellboy: The Lost Army*, a novel by Christopher Golden profusely illustrated by Hellboy's creator Mike Mignola [Dark Horse], *Maxon's Poe* (seven of Edgar Allan's tales as interpreted by by Robert's brother, Maxon Crumb [Word Play]), and *The Dark Tower IV: Wizard and Glass* by Stephen King (moodily illustrated by Dave McKean [Grant]).

FPG's aggressive move from trading cards into art book publishing came to a screeching halt with that company's sudden bankruptcy in the late summer. The future of the business was still in question by the end of the year and some creators began shopping their pro-

*Eric Nesheim's book colorfully explored the multi-generational pop-culture phenomenon of flying saucers and their alien pilots.*

jects to other publishers. Sirius Entertainment stepped in and midwifed Brom's monograph, *Darkwërks*, which quickly became one of the most popular and sought-after art volumes of the year. Justifiably so: Brom's instinctive ability and sly wit have made him one of the most interesting artists currently working.

FPG *was* able to release *Knightsbridge: The Art of Keith Parkinso*n and *Beyond Fantasy: The Art of Darrell K. Sweet* prior to their business difficulties. Speculation as of this writing is that FPG will be able to satisfy their creditors and reenter the market in the near future.

A happier note was HarperCollins' release of an unusual and welcome celebration of the gifted William Joyce (*The World of William Joyce Scrapbook*). A brilliant stylist and storyteller, Joyce also is incredibly funny (check out his "author photos") and this short retrospective, though marketed for kids, was the proverbial delight for children of all ages.

*The Art of Joe Chiodo* (WildStorm Productions) beautifully displayed the work of an under-appreciated talent: those familiar only with Chiodo's cute pin-up stylings were surprised at the breadth and depth of his range.

Conversely, Verotik's *Biz: The Intense Art of Simon Bisley*, while featuring some impressive illustrations, focused almost exclusively on that artist's works of cartoonish violence and perhaps clouded Bisley's originality and true artistic ability. But speaking of extremes, The King of Nightmarish Excess (his fans would be disappointed if he was otherwise), H.R. Giger was well represented both with the exhaustively superlative and bargain-priced *www.Giger.com* [Taschen] and the new edition of *H.R. Giger: 1964—1984* [James Cowan's Morpheus International].

Clyde Caldwell, widely popular for his work for TSR, produced *Savage Hearts: The Clyde Caldwell Sketchbook Vol. 1* (SalQ Productions); *Luz: The Art of Ciruelo* (Bast) was an appealing collection of Ciruelo Cabral's distinctive paintings, and Overlook published Rodney Matthew's latest collection, *Countdown to Millennium*. French airbrush artist Hubert de Lartigue had a selection of his fantasy-flavored pin-up art collected in *Heroines* (Solies) while Brit Dave McKean's influential art for DC was given an impressive showcase with *The Sandman: Dust Covers—The Collected Sandman Covers 1989-1996* (Vertigo). William Stout once again exhibited his drawing skills with *William Stout: The Dinosaurs Sketchbook* (Terra Nova), Olivia deBeradinis took another step toward securing her reputation as *the* pin-up artist of the '90s with *Second Slice: The Art of Olivia* (Ozone), Del Rey

produced *Star Wars: The Art of the Brothers Hildebrandt*, and Hajime Sorayama's latest collection, *Naga* (Shuppan Sha) was simultaneously titillating yet deeply disturbing. In a lighter vein were the latest retrospective compilation *Mad About the 50s*, and Al Jaffe's unique *Mad: Fold This Book* (both from Warner).

Vincent DiFate's long-anticipated illustrated history of science fiction art, *Infinite Worlds* (Penguin), was a beautifully ambitious attempt to codify a fragmented art field. Although some critics might justifiably argue that DiFate's personal preferences resulted in the exclusion of some important contributors or question his rather arbitrary definition of what makes one creator a "science fiction" artist and another a fantasist, such observations still do not diminish the importance or value of his book. The fact that *Infinite Worlds*, at long last, credits many artists who (though working in anonymity through much of their careers) changed the visual language of fantastic art and, albeit inadvertently, literature, would be reason enough to buy the volume.

A personal favorite in '97 was Ron Lesser's *Pulp Art* (Random House), a tremendous collection of all-but-forgotten paintings, newly separated from the originals and featuring some truly classic work. Similarly nostalgic was *Saucer Attack* by Eric Nesheim, packaged by Kitchen Sink for the General Publishing Group and featuring all manner of extraterrestrial paraphenalia and art. SalQ Productions continued with their bargain-priced "Gallery Girls" pin-up anthologies like *Amazon Empire*, *Dragontails*, and *Leather & Lace*, which included pencil art by Blas Gallegos, Fred Fields, Greg Loudon, Joe Chiodo, and a host of others.

Richard Kadrey's examination of the popular computer role-playing games, *From Myst to Riven* (Hyperion), Jerry Beck and Will Friedwald's *Warner Bros. Animation Art* (Warner), and *Walt Disney's Sleeping Beauty: The Sketchbook Series* (Applewood) all provided fascinatingly different perspectives on animation.

As with any year, there were a wide variety of film tie-ins, how-to books, and art annuals published both in the U.S. and abroad. And Bud Plant—whose business continues to grow at a rate that's the envy of Fortune 500 companies—remains as *the* single most reliable resource for all manner of illustrated and art-related books, both domestic and foreign. A sample catalog is available from Bud Plant Comic Art, P.O. Box 1689, Grass Valley, CA 95945-1689. (Phone: 530-273-2166/E-mail:cs@budplant.com/website: www.budplant.com.). You won't be disappointed.

## COMICS

If you enjoy angst, bitterness, persistent bickering, and utter frustration, the comic book industry in 1997 would have been just your cup of tea.

Still suffering in one way or another from an industry-wide sales slump that began slightly more than three-years ago, publishers, creators, and retailers spent more than a few sleepless nights wondering how they could turn things around while ignoring the obvious. Nostalgic for the heady days when

*Mike Mignola's funny and spooky* Hellboy *was easily one of 1997's most consistently worthwhile comics series.*

practically any title with characters sporting tights and a cape would sell a million copies and have Hollywood and toy companies banging down their doors, major publishers pumped more and more repetitive product into a dwindling market, ignoring variety in favor of increased brand-indentification. Alternative publishers scrambled to remain viable

*Illustrator Ron Lesser's popular* Pulp Art *featured arresting images from his own extensive collection as well as those of Jim Steranko and Danton Burroughs, among others.*

(usually with sex comics) as the interest in their products decreased, while retailers became more unwilling to take risks with inven-

*Perhaps the most artistically interesting project from the beleaguered Marvel Comics wasn't produced by Marvel at all:* Wizard *published this stunning futuristic "What If...?" premium by Alex Ross as a give-away.*

tory, creating their own version of *Catch-22* for the industry.

Indeed, it seemed that comic companies and their creators spent more time developing "concepts", gimmicks, and action figures than they did trying to tell stories. Everyone was scrambling to create the new *Men In Black* (or *Batman,* or *The Mask*), everybody wanted to have the next "hot" license so they could become media moguls, but ignored the fact that distribution outlets for their lines had diminished markedly. The corporate bean-counter-mentality married the delusional prima-donna flavor-of-the-week creator and conceived...a mess. The fun and sincerity of the art form has, at least for the time being, been replaced with laughable pretension and frighteningly desperate greed. It'll probably get worse before it gets better.

Does that mean there was nothing to recommend in the comics field in 1997? Of course not. There was plenty.

DC was once again the most interesting of the "Big Boy" publishers, with a wealth of creative talent and a diversity of concepts. Their fiddling with Superman's costume and powers got them the media attention they were calculating on, but didn't create the frenzy among collectors that the character's "death" generated a few years ago. Rather, the "must-have" item for fans was the Graphitti Designs-packaged *Kingdom Come* compila-

tion by Alex Ross and Mark Waid—a gorgeously-executed collectible that sold out prior to publication. Ross also beautifully illustrated Steve Darnall's mini-series *Uncle Sam*. Similarly, the single volume *Batman: Black & White* included all of the outstanding work I recommended in last year's *Spectrum* as well as an exceptional new cover by Jeffrey Jones. Hermann Mejia enthusiastically illustrated Alan Grant's script for *Lobo: Fragtastic Voyage,* Paul Lee provided effective graphics for *Hellblazer/The Books of Magic* #2 (written by Paul Jenkins and John Ney Rieber), writer/artist Ted McKeever defined edginess with *Junk Culture,* and Teddy Kristiansen eerily complimented Steven Seagle's stories for *House of Secrets.* Impressive covers included those by Chris Moeller (*Batman: Shadow of the Bat*), Michael William Kaluta (*Weird War* #2), Tim Bradstreet (*Unknown Soldier* #1), Joe Chiodo (*Nightwing Annual* #1), Brian Bolland (*The Invisibles*), Gary Gianni (*The Spectre* #52), Glen Fabry (*Preacher*), and Glen Orbik (*Superman Annual* #9). George Pratt, John Higgins, Daniel Brereton, Bruce Timm, and Richard Corben produced memorable additions to the DC universe.

As an umbrella publishing company for a diverse group of studios, Image Comics continued to mature and solidify its position in the industry. Todd McFarlane maintained the highest profile of the Image creators with his ongoing *Spawn* comics and its live-action film, toys, and HBO animated series spin-offs—certainly an enviable success story that unfortunately left McFarlane with less and less time at the drawing board. *Kurt Busiek's Astro City,* with art by Brent Anderson and covers by Alex Ross, received the field's highest accolades while Marc Silvestri's *Darkness* (written by Garth Ennis) rapidly became one of the year's hottest selling titles. Sam Kieth's *The Maxx,* Jae Lee's *Hellshock* and David Wenzel's *The Wizard's Tale* (written by Kurt Busiek) were all consistently well-done. But *the* artist to watch at Image clearly was Travis Charest (check out *WildC.A.T.S./X-Men* [written by Scott Lobdell], as well as various covers). Exhibiting strong compositional skills matched with a

natural drawing ability, Charest's work was fresh, energetic, and managed to stand out in Image's crowd of powerful talents.

Dark Horse Comics, another creator-friendly publisher, released a stack of noteworthy titles throughout the years. Though perhaps best-known for their tie-in series to films like *Alien, Star Wars,* and *Predator,* the real excitement was generated by their non-movie titles. Mike Mignola's wonderfully off-beat *Hellboy: Almost Colossus* and *Hellboy Christmas Special* (both with excellent back-up features by Gary Gianni) combined stunning graphics with carefully conceived stories. Barry Windsor-Smith battled comic-format prejudice from retailers and readers alike with his oversized *Storyteller* comics, a prejudice his intricate work seemingly couldn't overcome: Smith announced suspension of the series while he reconsidered the market's vagaries. Meanwhile, Ricardo Delgado continued to amaze with his wordless *Age of Reptiles: The Hunt,* Paola Parente and writer Warren Ellis

*Japan's Fewture Models, renowned for their intricate kits, produced another winner with Nina Darkness, a recurring character in their line.*

interpreted Robert Heinlein's *Starship Troopers,* and Steve "The Dude" Rude tackled the latest Nexus epic, *God Con 1* (written by Mike Baron). John Bolton, Daniel Brereton, Mark Schultz, Arthur Adams, and Den Beauvais were only some of the artists contributing exceptional work for a variety of titles.

Kitchen Sink Press, one of the most innovative of the alternative publishers, ran into a financial roadblock in early 1997 and was forced to temporarily suspend operations and cancel titles while they secured more stable financial backing. Back up and running within a matter of weeks of their crisis, they used the balance of the year to reevaluate their business plan and reenter the marketplace. Work of merit included Phil Hester's art for *The Crow: Waking Nightmares* (covers by Miran Kim), John Mueller's *Oink: Blood & Circus,* Charles Burns' *Black Hole,* and the ongoing *Li'l Abner* newspaper strip reprints by Al Capp and Frank Frazetta.

Sirius Entertainment released excellent work by Joseph Michael Lisner, Mark Crilley, David Mack, Jill Thompson, Voltaire, and Roel; Acclaim featured memorable art by Charles Adlard, Mike Evans, Ashley Wood, and Paul Gulacy; *Heavy Metal*'s 20th anniversary issue sported work by Scott Hampton, Luis Royo, and Caza; and Verotik published some knockout pieces by Dave Stevens, Joe Chiodo, Simon Bisley, and Arthur Suydam. A visit to the local comics shop revealed exceptional art by a lengthy list of creatives, including Chris Ware (*Acme Novelty Library*/Fantagraphics), Greg Spalinka (*Tales From the Edge*/Vanguard), Tom Simonton (*Amazon Woman Jungle Annual*/Fantaco), Rich Larson (*Demon Baby*/666 Comics), and Berni Wrightson (*Classic Monsters Nightmare Theatre*/Chaos), to name only a handful.

Although the comics industry is still sorely in need of a professional trade journal, there *are* several magazines that provide some needed insight to the field, including Gemstone's *Comic Book Marketplace*, Fantagraphics' contentious *The Comics Journal*, and *Wizard*, all available at better comic shops.

What 1998 will bring is surely anyone's guess: whatever unfolds, the one thing we can be assured of is that the comics field will be, if nothing else, interesting to watch.

## DIMENSIONAL

If any collectible art market experienced enviable growth in 1997 it was in the field of statues and models. There seemed to be a "chatchki" explosion as demand for figures ranging from Real Musgrave's modestly priced "Pocket Dragons" to $20,000 Armani porcelains grew by leaps and bounds. Warner Brothers' chain of stores featured a variety of fun offerings based on vintage cartoon characters while Disney aficionados were treated with limited editions based on their animated features, including a glorious demon from *Fantasia*'s "Night on Bald Mountain."

*Attractive and informative,* Amazing Figure Modeler *always is an interesting forum for the field's best sculptors.*

The Greenwich Workshop produced some breathtaking 3-D works based on the works for James C. Christensen and Scott Gustafson—truly exceptional craftsmanship at reasonable prices. Willits released an impressive line of figures in Thomas Blackshear II's Ebony Visions line, while Randy Bowen kept busy with his series of fantasy busts (one of 1997's was based on Moebius' Arzach character). The Shiflett Brothers team created an

awesomely proportioned "Draco" (from the film *Dragonheart*) and "Duke Nukem" (from the computer game) for Moore Creations as well as a triumphant "Jaguar God" for Verotik. Shawn Nagle released the "Stoutosaurus," based on William Stout's 1982 designs for an aborted Godzilla film, and the humorous "Miss Giger Girl" (Nagleworks); Simian Productions produced "Little Miss Muffit" and "Grafter" (based on paintings by Brom) along with the wicked "Devil Girls" (inspired by the underground art of "Coop"), all sculpted by Barsom Manashian; and DC continued with their line of William Paquet-sculpted figures, with perhaps the best being "Preacher," based on Glenn Fabry art. *Spectrum* reader Gail Seaton Humbert called my attention to the enchanting work of British sculptor Andrew Bill for Holland Studio Craft Limited, a division of Royal Doulton. Bill's offerings in '97 included a pair of dragons ("Leviathan" and "Confrontation"), and two female figures, "Spring Witch Bruntian" and "Sumer [sic] Witch Vijian."

Other dimensional art worth mentioning in 1997 included "Iria" by Kazuo Uragashira, Thomas Kuntz's "Bela Lugosi: King of Vampires" (Dark Horse), "Animal Mystic" (designed by Dark One and sculpted by Susumu Sugita for Sirius), "God of the Robots" (based on a painting by Kelly Freas: sculpted by Mat Falls), Tony McVey's reinterpretation/updating of Ray Harryhausen's "Ymir" '50s movie monster, and the stunning "Nina Darkness," the most recent addition in an ongoing series sculpted by Yuji Oniki for Japan's Fewture Models.

There are several slick magazines that help keep track of the evolving field of fantasy statues and limited edition models: *Amazing Figure Modeler* (Dept. 10, P.O. Box 30885, Columbus, OH 43230/sample $7.00) and *Kitbuilders* (Gordy's, Box 201, Sharon, OH 44274-1657/sample $6.00) are two of the best sources currently available.

## INSTITUTIONAL

It isn't a startling revelation that fantastic art continued to crop up in a wide range of expected and unexpected venues, products, and galleries; so many in fact that it is virtually impossible to do anything other than list a very few of the "institutional" offerings that caught my attention in '97. Noted were James Gurney's dinosaur stamps and Thomas Blackshear II's Universal Monster tribute stamps for the Post Office; Graphitti Designs' *Roswell* fridge magnets by Bill Morrison and James Bama's "Doc Savage" prints, *Green Death* and *Cold Death*; the Greenwich Workshop's ongoing line of Scott Gustafson's ex-

pressive fairy tale prints; Comic Images's trading cards (Royo, *Martian School Girls* by Paul Pope, and *Ghost*); Wildstorm's character stickers, Gen 13 magnets, and *Savage Dragon*

*Thomas Blackshear II produced a wonderful tribute to Bela Lugosi, Boris Karloff, and the Chaney's (Jr. and Sr.) with a stamp series for the post office. The images were also offered on T-shirts and magnets.*

trading cards; and Sirius' *Scary Godmother* greeting cards by Jill Thompson, Brom's *Tombstone Girls* portfolio, and *The Book of Ballads & Sagas* folio by Charles Vess. There was the usual eye-catching selection of calendars (including those featuring Frank Frazetta, H.R. Giger, Boris Vallejo, and William Joyce), posters (Kent Williams' "Destiny" for DC was a standout), plates, action figures (Moore creations produced exceptional work), and film design (Moebius' contributions to *The 5th Element* were original and refreshing).

There were countless exhibitions at galleries and conventions around the country, including major shows by Michael Whelan at Tree's Place in Orleans, Massachusetts, Joe Kubert at the Words & Pictures Museum in Northampton, MA (a *great* facility!), and Kent Williams at the now sadly closed 4 Color Images in New York

Artist Brigid Marlin was one of the founders of an annual exhibition in London entitled "The Art of Imagination" that is closely linked with the Museum for Fantastic & Visionary Art in Vienna, Austria. Artists interested in more information can contact the society for Art of the Imagination at P.O. Box 240, Berkhamsted, Herts. H.P.4 1SS, U.K. or can phone/fax Brigid at 01442864454.

Finally, collectors of original art again had a number of places to shop, including conventions, website galleries, and directly from some artists. Three reliable resources for fantastic works are Jane Frank's venerable Worlds of Wonder (P.O. Box 814, McLean, VA 22101[703-847-4251/website: http//www.wow-art.com]), Illustration House (96 Spring St., 7th Floor, New York, NY 10012-3923 [212-966-9444]), and Scott Dunbier's Wildstorm Fine Arts (phone: 619-551-9724 or fax at 619-551-9544/website: wsfa@wildstorm.com). Check them out.    †

SPECTRUM 1997
Call For Entries Poster
*Art & Concept:*
**GARY RUDDELL**

*artist:* **EZRA TUCKER**
*art director:* **Harold Tackett & Krista Dietz**    *client:* **World Com/Wiltel**    *title:* **Life's a Breeze With Wiltel**
*size:* **15"x20"**    *medium:* **acylic**

**1**
*artist:* **MARC GABBANA**
*title:* Robot Wars 1997
*medium:* Acrylic
*size:* 211/2"x17"

**2**
*artist:* **MARC SASSO**
*art director:* Sean Kyne
*client:* Mattel Toys
*medium:* Acrylic
*size:* 12"x12"

**3**
*artist:* **EZRA TUCKER**
*art director:* Harold Tackett & Krista Dietz
*client:* World Com/Wiltel
*title:* Dive In With Wiltel
*medium:* Acrylic
*size:* 15"x20"

**4**
*artist:* **MARGARET ORGAN-KEAN**
*digital artist:* Dave Howell
*art director:* Dave Howell
*client:* Alexandria Digital Literature
*title:* Alexandria Poster—1998
*medium:* Watercolor/digital
*size:* 13"x17"

1

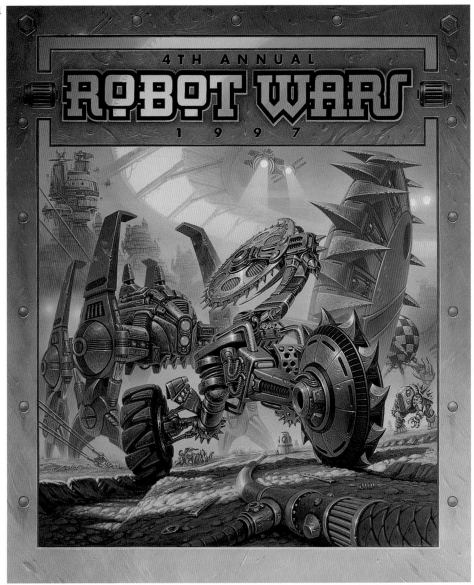

2

3

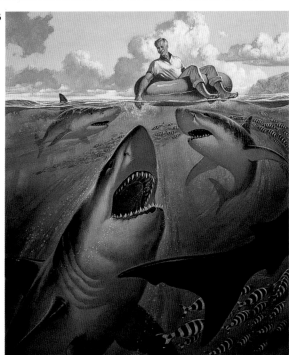

4

**1**
*artist:* **RAFAL OLBINSKI**
*client:* Arizona Theatre Company   *title:* Picasso   *medium:* Acrylic

**2**
*artist:* **KEN MEYER JR.**
*art director:* Ken Meyer Jr.   *client:* Lacunae Magazine   *title:* The First Taste
*medium:* Acrylic   *size:* 12"x12"

**3**
*artist:* **DAVID DEVRIES**
*art director:* Tom Carling   *client:* Topps, Inc.   *title:* Princess Leia
*medium:* Mixed   *size:* 20"x30"

**4**
*artist:* **RAFAL OLBINSKI**
*client:* National Arts Club   *title:* Olbinski Exhibition   *medium:* Acrylic

**1**
*artist:* **MARC GABBANA**
*client:* S.O.D.
*title:* Aprönstrings
*medium:* Acrylic
*size:* 15"x15"

**2**
*artist:* **ROBH RUPPEL**
*art director:* Brent Millar
*client:* FPG
*medium:* Oil
*size:* 15"x20"

**3**
*artist:* **MARC SASSO**
*art director:* Marc Sasso
*client:* Thunder Force Entertainment
*title:* Wings of Prosthesis
*medium:* Acrylic/oil
*size:* 12 1/2"x16 1/4"

**4**
*artist:* **PATRICK ARRASMITH**
*art director:* Mimi Duvall
*designer:* Mimi Duvall
*client:* New York Law Journal
*title:* Millennium Bug
*medium:* Scraperboard
*size:* 8"x10"

1

2

3

4

artist: DAVE McKEAN
art director: Robert Weiner    designer: Dave McKean    client: Donald M. Grant/Publisher
title: Stephen King's Wizard & Glass: The Dark Tower IV    size: 61/4"x9"    medium: Mixed/digital

LOOK OUT, BIRD!

*artist:* RICHARD BERNAL
*art director:* James Barwick    *client:* Harcourt Brace    *title:* Catalog K-8
*size:* 17"x22"    *medium:* Oil

**1**
*artist:* **CHRIS MOORE**
*art director:* Madeline Meckiffe
*client:* Harper Collins
*title:* The Cosmic Puppets
*medium:* Acrylic
*size:* 21"x151/2"

**2**
*artist:* **NICK STATHOPOULOS**
*art director:* Nick Stathopoulos
*client:* Harper Collins
*title:* Ascension 1
*medium:* Oil
*size:* 24"x311/2"

**3**
*artist:* **BRUCE JENSEN**
*art director:* Irene Gallo
*client:* Tor Books
*title:* Frameshift
*medium:* Acrylic
*size:* 12"x17"

**4**
*artist:* **RICK BERRY**
*art director:* Arnie Fenner
*designer:* Arnie Fenner
*client:* Underwood Books
*title:* 11th Hour
*medium:* Mixed/digital

1

2

3

4

1
*artist:* **DON MAITZ**
*art director:* Jane Johnson
*client:* Harper Collins
*title:* Dragons On the Sea of Night
*medium:* Oil on masonite
*size:* 22"x30"

2
*artist:* **LES EDWARDS**
*art director:* Judy Lineard
*client:* Kingfisher Books
*title:* Fantasy Stories
*medium:* Oils
*size:* 12"x18"

3
*artist:* **ROMAS**
*art director:* Carl Galian
*client:* Penguin USA
*title:* Allamanda
*medium:* Acrylic
*size:* 15"x23"

4
*artist:* **DiTERLIZZI**
*art director:* Aileen Miles
*client:* White Wolf Publishing
*title:* Land of 8 Million Dreams
*medium:* Watercolor/gouache
*size:* 20"x30"

4

20229186

**1**
*artist:* **JOHN HARRIS**
*art director:* Irene Gallo
*client:* Tor Books
*title:* The Other End of Time 2
*medium:* Oils
*size:* 20"x13"

**2**
*artist:* **JOHN JUDE PALENCAR**
*art director:* George Cornell
*designer:* George Cornell
*client:* Penguin USA
*title:* The Regulators/Desperation
*medium:* Acrylic
*size:* 15"x20"

**3**
*artist:* **JOHN ZELEZNIK**
*client:* Palladium Books
*title:* Rifts Lone Star
*medium:* Acrylic
*size:* 18"x24"

**4**
*artist:* **ŻELJKO PAHEK**
*client:* Prosveta
*title:* Philip K. Dick's Ubik
*medium:* Gouache
*size:* 8"x12"

**5**
*artist:* **PAUL YOULL**
*art director:* Jamie Warren Youll
*designer:* Paul Youll
*client:* Bantam Books
*title:* The Multiplex Man
*medium:* Acrylic/oil
*size:* 19 1/2"x27"

**6**
*artist:* **BOB EGGLETON**
*art director:* Stephen Jones
*client:* World Fantasy Con '97
*title:* Gorgzillicus
*medium:* Acrylic
*size:* 18"x24"

1

2

3

4

5

6

**1**

*artist:* **JIM BURNS**
*art director:* Liz Laczynska
*client:* Transworld
*title:* To Hold Infinity
*medium:* Oils
*size:* 28"x21"

**2**

*artist:* **PHIL HALE**
*art director:* Richard Thomas
*client:* White Wolf Publishing
*title:* Elric: Song of the Black Sword
*medium:* Oils

**3**

*artist:* **DAVE McKEAN**
*art director:* Robert Weiner
*designer:* Dave McKean
*client:* Donald M. Grant Books
*title:* Dark Tower IV
*medium:* Mixed/digital
*size:* 6 1/4"x9"

**4**

*artist:* **BRUCE JENSEN**
*art director:* Judith Murello
*client:* Berkley Publishing Group
*title:* Faraday's Orphans
*medium:* Acrylic
*size:* 15"x20"

**1**

**2**

**3**

4

**1**
*artist:* **WILLIAM JOYCE**

**2**
*artist:* **WILLIAM JOYCE**

**3**
*artist:* **CIRUELO**
*art director:* Ciruelo
*designer:* Ciruelo
*client:* Ciruelo
*title:* King's Demon
*medium:* Acrylic
*size:* 10"x14"

**4**
*artist:* **MARK A. NELSON**
*art director:* James Nelson
*client:* Fasa Corporation
*title:* Drone
*medium:* Acrylic
*size:* 101/2"x131/2"

**1**
*artist:* **JANNY WURTS**
*art director:* Gene Mydlowski
*client:* Harper Collins
*title:* Fugitive Prince
*medium:* Oils   *size:* 36"x23 1/2"

**2**
*artist:* **MARK A. NELSON**
*art director:* T. Bradstreet
*client:* Myrmidon Press
*title:* Dark Angle 1
*medium:* Pencil   *size:* 9 3/4"x13"

**3**
*artist:* **GREGORY MANCHESS**
*art director:* Nancy Leo
*client:* Dial Books
*title:* Malcolm: Pirate King
*medium:* Oil on canvas

**4**
*artist:* **R.K. POST**
*art director:* Dawn Murin
*client:* TSR
*title:* The Great Modron March
*medium:* Oils   *size:* 18"x24"

**1**

**2**

**3**

4

**1**
*artist:* **SAVIC BOBAN**
*art director:* Geto
designer: Geto
*medium:* Gouache
*size:* 6"x9"

**2**
*artist:* **ROMAS**
*art director:* Sheila Gilbert
*client:* Daw Books
*title:* Razor's Edge
*medium:* Acrylic
*size:* 17"x28"

**3**
*artist:* **CHRIS MOORE**
*art director:* Madeline Meckiffe
*client:* Harper Collins
*title:* The Zap Gun
*medium:* Acrylic
*size:* 151/2"x21"

**4**
*artist:* **NICHOLAS JAINSCHIGG**
*art director:* Irene Gallo
*client:* Tor Books
*title:* Signs of Life
*medium:* Acrylic
*size:* 18"x24"

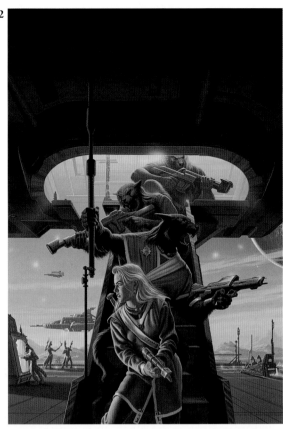

4

**1**
*artist:* **JIM BURNS**
*art director:* Jamie Warren Youll
*client:* Bantam Books
*title:* Heaven's Reach
*medium:* Oils

**2**
*artist:* **GARY GIANNI**
*client:* Wandering Star
*title:* The Savage Tales of Solomon Kane
*medium:* Pen & ink
*size:* 5"x12"

**3**
*artist:* **GARY GIANNI**
*client:* Wandering Star
*title:* The Savage Tales of Solomon Kane
*medium:* Pen & ink
*size:* 15"x22"

**4**
*artist:* **GARY GIANNI**
*client:* Wandering Star
*title:* The Savage Tales of Solomon Kane
*medium:* Oils
*size:* 22"x36"

4

**1**
*artist:* **DEAN MORRISSEY**
*designer:* Darilyn Carnes/
Dean Morrissey
*client:* Harry N. Abrams
*title:* The Wooden Swan
(Mother Nature)
*medium:* Oils
*size:* 48"x36"

**2**
*artist:* **MICHAEL DASHOW**
*art director:* Michael Dashow
*client:* Tachyon Publications
*title:* The Rhinoseros Who
Quoted Nietesche
*medium:* Pencil/digital

**3**
*artist:* **JILL BAUMAN**
*art director:* Alan Dingman
*client:* St. Martin's Press
*title:* The Star of India
*medium:* Acrylic
*size:* 14"x20"

**4**
*artist:* **GREG NEWBOLD**
*art director:* Golda Lavrens
*client:* Beechtree Books
*title:* Witch Week
*medium:* Acrylic
*size:* 8"x12"

**1**

**3**

**2**

4

NEWBOLD

**1**
*artist:* **BARCLAY SHAW**
*designer:* Irene Gallo
*client:* Tor Books
*title:* Nano Flower
*medium:* Digital

**2**
*artist:* **GYORGY KORGA**

**3**
*artist:* **RON WALOTSKY**
*art director:* Richard Hasselberge
*client:* Penguin Roc
*title:* Gate of Ivory/
Gate of Horn
*medium:* Acrylic
*size:* 15"x20"

**4**
*artist:* **LES EDWARDS**
*art director:* Jim Nelson
*client:* FASA Corporation
*title:* Rigger Sourcebook
*medium:* Oils
*size:* 16"x18"

1

2

3

**1**
*artist:* **JOHN JUDE PALENCAR**
*art director:* Judith Murello
*designer:* John Jude Palencar & Judith Murello
*client:* Berkley Books
*title:* Jovah's Angel
*medium:* Acrylic
*size:* 27"x29"

**2**
*artist:* **JOHN JUDE PALENCAR**
*art director:* Rich Hasselberger
*designer:* John Jude Palencar & Rich Hasselberger
*client:* Penguin U.S.A.
*title:* The Drawing of the Three
*medium:* Acrylic
*size:* 18"x20"

**3**
*artist:* **BRUCE JENSEN**
*art director:* Judith Murello
*client:* Berkley Books
*title:* Forever Peace
*medium:* Acrylic
*size:* 16"x22"

**4**
*artist:* **JOHN JUDE PALENCAR**
*art director:* Rich Hasselberger
*designer:* John Jude Palencar & Rich Hasselberger
*client:* Penguin U.S.A.
*title:* The Wastelands
*medium:* Acrylic
*size:* 18"x20"

**1**

**2**

**3**

4

**1**
*artist:* **CHARLES KEEGAN**
*art director:* Dave Stevenson    *client:* Del Rey Books
*title:* Tarzan and the Golden Lion
*medium:* Oil on canvas    *size:* 25"x30"
Tarzan copyright © 1997 Edgar Rice Burroughs, Inc.

**2**
*artist:* **JOHN HOWE**
*art director:* Jane Johnson    *designer:* Erika Brewer
*client:* Harper Collins    *title:* Mythago Wood
*medium:* Watercolor    *size:* 29"x22"

**3**
*artist:* **BOBAN ŚAVIC**
*art director:* Geto    *designer:* Geto    *medium:* Pen & ink    *size:* 5"x8"

3

GETO

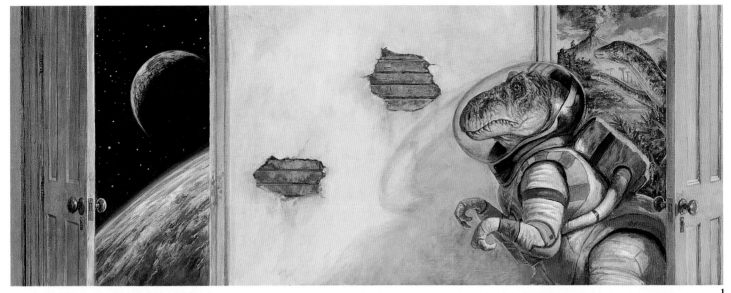

1

2

3

1
*artist:* **BOB EGGLETON**
*art director:* Jim Kelly
*designer:* Jim Turner
*client:* Golden Gryphon Press
*title:* Think Like a Dinosaur
*medium:* Acrylic
*size:* 29"x14"

2
*artist:* **DANIEL R. HORNE**
*art director:* Stephen Daniele
*client:* T.S.R.
*title:* World Builder's Guide
*medium:* Oil on masonite
*size:* 18"x24"

3
*artist:* **TRISTAN ELWELL**
*art director:* Lisa Peters
*client:* Harcourt Brace
*title:* Curses, Inc.
*medium:* Oil
*size:* 11 1/2"x17"

4
*artist:* **GREG HARLIN**
*art director:* Paul Buckley
*client:* Penguin U.S.A.
*title:* The Bad Samaritan
*medium:* Acrylic
*size:* 11"x14"

4

**1**
*artist:* **STEPHEN YOULL**
*art director:* Jamie Warren
*designer:* Stephen Youll
*client:* Bantam Books
*title:* A Clash of Kings
*medium:* Oils   *size:* 17"x24"

**2**
*artist:* **D. ALEXANDER GREGORY**
*art director:* Larry Snelly
*client:* Whitewolf Publishing
*title:* Renegades
*medium:* Mixed   *size:* 10"x14"

**3**
*artist:* **CLYDE CALDWELL**
*art director:* Clyde Caldwell
*designer:* Grassy Knoll Studios
*client:* SQ Productions
*title:* The Leopard & The Serpent
*medium:* Oils   *size:* 16"x20½"

**4**
*artist:* **GREGORY MANCHESS**
*art director:* Nancy Leo
*client:* Dial Books
*title:* Conagh
*medium:* Oil on canvas

**1**

artist: **RICHARD BERNAL**
art director: Richard Bernal
client: Publications International
title: Rikki-Tikki-Tavi
medium: Acrylic   size: 9"x11"

**2**

artist: **ROBERT CRUMB**
art director: C. Evan Metcalf
designer: Peter Poplaski
client: Kitchen Sink Press/Little Brown
title: The R. Crumb Coffee Table Art Book
medium: Ink & watercolor

**3**

artist: **TODD LOCKWOOD**
art director: Dawn Murin
client: T.S.R., Inc.
title: Ghost
medium: Oils   size: 17"x24"

**4**

artist: **JON FOSTER**
art director: Jason Hawkins
designer: Jon Foster
client: Iron Crown Enterprises
title: Quarrying
medium: Acrylic   size: 14"x17"

**1**

**2**

**3**

4

**1**
*artist:* **WILLIAM JOYCE**
*client:* Laura Geringer Books/HarperCollins
*title:* The Leaf Men

**2**
*artist:* **JOSEPH DeVITO**
*art director:* Charles Kochman
*client:* DC Comics/Prima Publishing
*title:* Wonder Woman: Gods & Goddesses
*medium:* Oil   *size:* 16"x20"
Wonder Woman ™ and copyright © 1998 DC Comics. All Rights Reserved.

**3**
*artist:* **DONATO GIANCOLA**
*art director:* Ray Lundgren
*client:* Penguin/Roc
*title:* Godheads
*medium:* Oil   *size:* 15"x22"

**4**
*artist:* **DONATO GIANCOLA**
*art director:* Carl Galian
*client:* Penguin/Roc
*title:* Mars At Jupiter
*medium:* Oil   *size:* 14"x22"

4

**1**

*artist:* **THOMAS M. BAXA**
*art director:* Neil Darcy    *client:* Ronin Publishing
*title:* Be One With the Sacred Seal    *medium:* Oils    *size:* 30"x37"

**2**

*artist:* **RICHARD BOBER**
*art director:* Allison Williams    *client:* Tor Books
*title:* Cross and Crescent    *medium:* Acrylic & oils    *size:* 22"x30"

**3**

*artist:* **ROBH RUPPEL**
*art director:* Dawn Murin    *client:* T.S.R., Inc.    *title:* Harbinger House
*medium:* Oils    *size:* 20"x30"

**4**

*artist:* **MARK ELLIOTT**
*art director:* Nick Krenitsky    *client:* HarperCollins    *title:* Ella Enchanted
*medium:* Acrylic    *size:* 15"x20"

**1**

**2**

**3**

4

*artist:* **TRAVIS CHAREST**

*art director:* **Scott Dunbier**    *client:* **Wildstorm Productions**    *title:* **Wildcore #1 [Variant Cover]**    *size:* **11"x17"**    *medium:* Mix

artist: VINCENT EVANS

art director: Fabian Nicieza     client: Acclaim Comics     title: Shadow Man

size: 20"x30"     medium: Oil

**1**

*artist:* **ALEXANDER MALEEV**
*art director:* Amie Brockway    *designer:* Lisa Stone
*client:* Kitchen Sink Press/Top Dollar Comics
*title:* The Crow: Dead Time Collection    *medium:* Ink & watercolor

**2**

*artist:* **JIM LEE**
*art director:* Rachelle Brissendski    *client:* Wildstorm Productions
*title:* Divine Right #2/P. 9    *medium:* Pencil & ink    *size:* 11"x17"

**3**

*artist:* **CHARLES BURNS**
*designer:* Chris Shadoian    *client:* Kitchen Sink Press    *title:* Black Hole #4
*medium:* Ink & gouache

**4**

*artist:* **CHRISTOPHER MOELLER**
*art director:* Dennis O'Neil    *client:* DC Comics
*title:* Shadow of the Bat #71    *medium:* Acrylic    *size:* 20"x30"

Batman is ™ and copyright © 1998 by DC Comics. All Rights Reserved.

**1**

**2**

**3**

**1**
*artist:* **VINCENT EVANS**
*art director:* Fabian Nicieza
*client:* Acclaim Comics
*title:* Ninjak
*medium:* Oils   *size:* 20"x30"

**2**
*artist:* **JOSEPH MICHAEL LINSNER**
*art director:* Joseph Michael Linsner
*client:* Sirius Entertainment
*title:* Dawn Five
*medium:* Mixed   *size:* 12"x17"

**3**
*artist:* **JOE JUSKO**
*art director:* Mark Mazz
*title:* Vampirella/Bloodlust
*medium:* Acrylic   *size:* 13"x20"

**4**
*artist:* **GREG LOUDON**
*art director:* Hart Fisher
*client:* Boneyard Press
*title:* Vampire Lust #2
*medium:* Acrylic   *size:* 15"x20"

1

2

3

4

1

1

2

3

**1**

*artist:* **TRAVIS CHAREST**
*art director:* Scott Dunbier
*client:* Wildstorm Productions
*title:* WildC.A.T.S./X-Men:
The Golden Age, P. 25
*medium:* Mixed   *size:* 11"x17"

**2**

*artist:* **STEVE RUDE**
*client:* Dark Horse Comics
*title:* God-Con One
*medium:* Oils   *size:* 20"x30"

**3**

*artist:* **CHRISTOPHER MOELLER**
*art director:* Dennis O'Neil
*client:* DC Comics
*title:* Shadow of the Bat #61
*medium:* Acrylic   *size:* 20"x30"

**4**

*artist:* **DOUG BEEKMAN**
*art director:* Mark Chiarello
*client:* DC Comics
*title:* Catwoman Annual
*medium:* Watercolor   *size:* 20"x24"

**1**

*artist:* **JOE JUSKO**
*art director:* Joe Jusko    *client:* Frank Frazetta Fantasy Illustrated    *title:* Hellriders
*medium:* Acrylic    *size:* 11"x17"

**2**

*artist:* **PAOLO PARENTE**
*art director:* Joe Andreani    *designer:* Paolo Parente    *client:* Marvel Comics
*title:* Conan: The Return of Styrm    *medium:* Oils & acrylic    *size:* 16"x24"

**3**

*artist:* **JOE JUSKO**
*art director:* Joe Jusko    *client:* Frank Frazetta Fantasy Illustrated    *title:* Hellriders
*medium:* Acrylic    *size:* 11"x17"

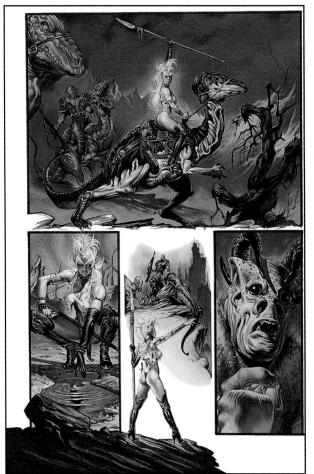

5

4

**4**
*artist:* **DAVE FIRCH/BATT/STEVE FIRCHOW**
*art director:* Marc Silvestri   *client:* Top Cow Productions   *title:* Grigorieff
*medium:* Mixed/digital   *size:* 11"x17"

**5**
*artist:* **STEVE ELLIS**
*client:* Unstoppable Productions   *title:* Tranquility   *medium:* Pencil & ink   *size:* 11"x17"

**5**
*artist:* **OMAHA PÉREZ**
*client:* Slave Labor Graphics   *title:* Raw Periphery   *medium:* Acrylic   *size:* 11"x15 1/2"

6

**1**

*artist:* **DEAN ARMSTRONG** [PAINTER] **& MIKE PASCALE** [PENCILS]
*art director:* Mike Pascale   *client:* Schism Comics   *title:* The Collected Bru-Hed
*medium:* Digital   *size:* 101/2"x133/4"

Bru-Head is ™ and copyright © 1998 by Schism Comics. All Rights Reserved.

**2**

*artist:* **GREG SPALENKA**
*art director:* David Spurlock   *designer:* David Spurlock   *client:* Tales From the Edge
*title:* Manifestation   *medium:* Mixed/digital   *size:* 8"x12"

**3**

*artist:* **PAUL CHADWICK**
*art director:* Randy Stradley   *client:* Dark Horse Comics   *title:* Strange Armor
*medium:* Acrylic & colored pencil   *size:* 11"x17"

**4**

*artist:* **PAUL CHADWICK**
*art director:* Randy Stradley   *client:* Dark Horse Comics   *title:* Strange Armor
*medium:* Acrylic & colored pencil   *size:* 11"x17"

**1**

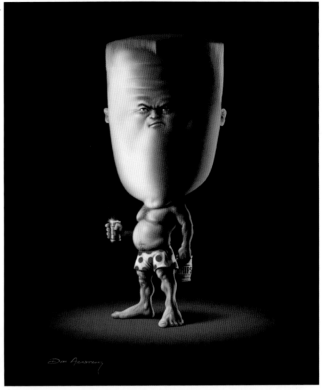

**2**

**3**

4

**1**

*artist:* **MARK CRILLEY**

*art director:* Joe Linsner   *designer:* Mark Crilley   *client:* Sirius Entertainment
*title:* Akiko [#14 Back Cover]   *medium:* Ink & watercolor   *size:* 10"x16"

**2**

*artist:* **JOHN MUELLER**

*art director:* Amie Brockway   *designer:* Kevin Lison   *client:* Kitchen Sink Press
*title:* Oink: Heaven's Butcher Collection   *medium:* Oil on board

**3**

*artist:* **CHRISTOPHER MOELLER**

*art director:* Dennis O'Neil   *client:* DC Comics   *title:* Shadow of the Bat #70
*medium:* Acrylic   *size:* 20"x30"

Batman is ™ and copyright© 1998 by DC Comics. All Rights Reserved.

**4**

*artist:* **BARRY WINDSOR-SMITH**

*art director:* Barry Windsor-Smith   *designer:* Barry Windsor-Smith
*client:* Barry Windsor-Smith: Storyteller   *title:* Princess Adastra
*medium:* Ink, color pencil & watercolor   *size:* 7"x12 1/2"

4

**1**
*artist:* **STEVE FIRCHOW**
*art director:* Tim Herriandez   *client:* Top Cow Productions   *title:* The Darkness
*medium:* Oils   *size:* 10"x14"

**2**
*artist:* **JON J. MUTH**
*art director:* Shelly Roeberg   *designer:* Richard Bruning   *client:* DC/Vertigo Comics
*title:* Farewell Moonshadow   *medium:* Watercolor   *size:* 81/2"x13"

**3**
*artist:* **MIRAN KIM**
*art director:* Amie Brockway   *designer:* Lisa Stone
*client:* Kitchen Sink Press/Top Dollar Comics   *title:* The Crow: Waking Nightmares #1
*medium:* Mixed

**4**
*artist:* **JOHN MUELLER**
*art director:* Amie Brockway   *designer:* C. Evan Metcalf
*client:* Kitchen Sink Press/Top Dollar Comics   *title:* The Crow: WILD JUSTICE #3
*medium:* Mixed

**1**

*artist:* **BROM**

*art director:* Brian Pulido   *designer:* Brom   *client:* Chaos Comics

*title:* Lady Death   *medium:* Oils

Lady Death and Evil Ernie are ™ and copyright © 1998 by Chaos Comics

**2**

*artist:* **JILL THOMPSON**

*art director:* Joe Linsner   *designer:* Jill Thompson   *client:* Sirius Entertainment

*title:* Scary Godmother   *medium:* Watercolor   *size:* 30"x20"

**3**

*artist:* **JOSEPH MICHAEL LINSNER**

*art director:* Joseph Michael Linsner   *designer:* Joseph Michael Linsner

*client:* Sirius Entertainment   *title:* Dawn One   *medium:* Mixed   *size:* 12"x17"

**1**

**2**

1
*artist:* **ALEX ROSS**
*art director:* Jonathan Peterson   *client:* Homage Comics   *title:* Astro City #11 Cover
*medium:* Watercolor   *size:* 12"x18"

2
*artist:* **ADAM HUGHES**
*art director:* Scott Dunbier   *client:* Wildstorm Productions   *title:* Voodoo #2 Cover
*medium:* Mixed   *size:* 11"x17"

3
*artist:* **STEVE RUDE**
*title:* Patricide   *medium:* Cel-Vinyl Acrylic   *size:* 20"x30"

4
*artist:* **MARC SILVESTRI/BATT/STEVE FIRCHOW**
*art director:* David Wohl   *client:* Top Cow Productions   *title:* The Darkness and Friends
*medium:* Pencil, ink & digital   *size:* 11"x17"

1

2

3

4

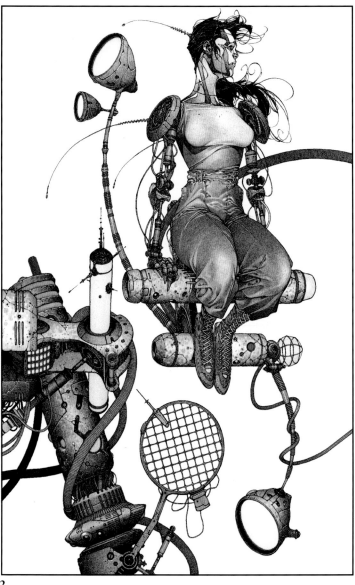

1

2

**1**

*artist:* **TRAVIS CHAREST**

*art director:* Scott Dunbier    *client:* Wildstorm Productions    *title:* DV8 #14 [Variant Cover]

*medium:* Mixed    *size:* 11"x17"

**2**

*artist:* **TRAVIS CHAREST**

*art director:* Scott Dunbier    *client:* Wildstorm Productions    *title:* Wetworks #32 [Variant Cover]

*medium:* Mixed    *size:* 11"x17"

**3**

*artist:* **STEVE RUDE**

*client:* DC Comics    *title:* Wonder Woman #1 Cover    *medium:* Oils    *size:* 20"x30"

Wonder Woman is ™ and copyright © 1998 by DC Comics. All Rights Reserved.

3

*sculptor:* **LAWRENCE NORTHEY**
*title:* **Chantecler Eldrorado (The Game Master)**     *size:* **28"Wx36"H**     *medium:* **Metal**

*sculptor:* **THE SHIFLETT BROS.**

*art director:* **Clay Moore**    *client:* **Moore Creations**    *title:* **Draco**    *size:* **12"Hx21"W**    *medium:* **Resin**

**1**
*sculptor:* **THE SHIFLETT BROS.**
*art director:* Glen Danzig
*designer:* Simon Bisley
*client:* Verotik
*title:* Jaguar God
*medium:* Resin
*size:* 11"H

**2**
*sculptor:* **KEVIN JOHNSON/ DON CLAVETTE**
*art director:* Scott Gustafson
*designer:* Scott Gustafson
*client:* The Greenwich Workshop
*title:* Humpty Dumpty
*medium:* Painted Resin
*size:* 7"H

**3**
*artist:* **JOSEPH DeVITO**
*art director:* Coyne Com.
*designer:* Joseph DeVito
*client:* Land Rover International
*medium:* Bronze
*size:* 24"Hx15"W

**4**
*sculptor:* **KEVIN JOHNSON**
*art director:* Scott Gustafson
*designer:* Scott Gustafson
*client:* The Greenwich Workshop
*title:* Humpty Dumpty
*medium:* Painted Resin
*size:* 61/2"H

**5**
*artist:* **JAMES CHRISTENSEN**
*client:* The Greenwich Workshop
*title:* The Bassoonist
*medium:* Porcelain
*size:* 71/4"H

1

2

3

4

5

**1**
*sculptor:* **KEVIN JOHNSON/
DON CLAVETTE/
SCOTT GUSTAFSON**
*art director:* Scott Gustafson
*designer:* Scott Gustafson
*client:* The Greenwich Workshop
*title:* Little Red Riding Hood &
The Wolf
*medium:* Painted Resin   *size:* 7"H

**2**
*sculptor:* **LAURA REYNOLDS**
*title:* Serpent Safari
*medium:* Mixed Media
*size:* 101/2"Wx111/2"H

**3**
*sculptor:* **SUSUMU SUGITA**
*art director:* Dark One
*designer:* Randy Bowen
*client:* Sirius Entertainment
*medium:* Cold-Cast Resin
*size:* 12"H

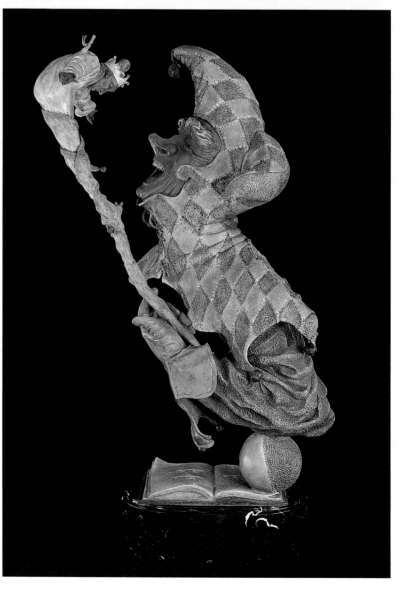

**4**
*sculptor:* **J.A. PIPPETT**
*title:* Wixten & Fig   *medium:* Bronze   *size:* 371/2"H

**5**
*sculptor:* **J.A. PIPPETT**
*title:* A Little Moonlight Reading   *medium:* Bronze   *size:* 171/4"H

5

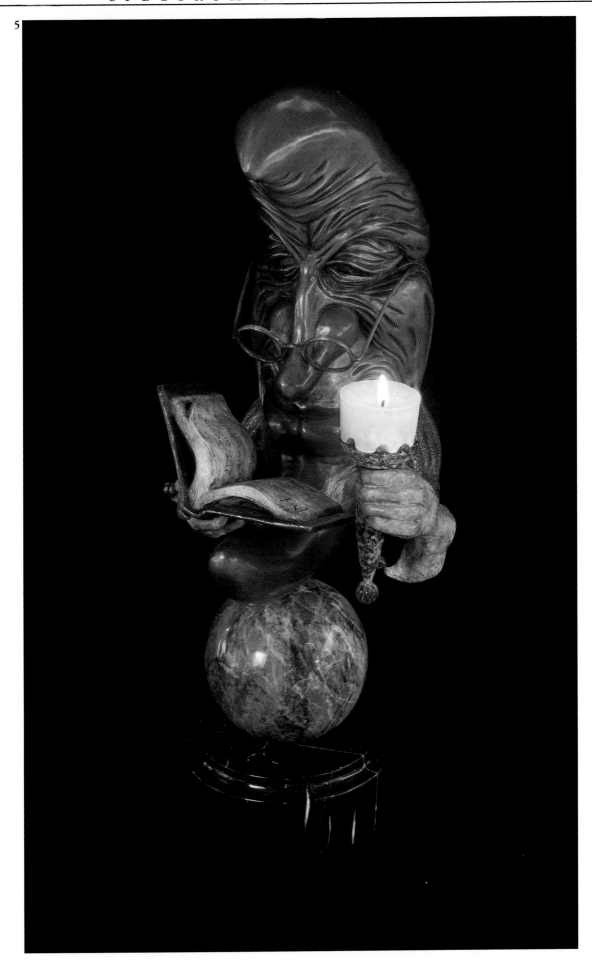

**1**

*sculptor:* **CLAYBURN S. MOORE**
*art director:* Clayburn S. Moore & Pul F. Moore
*title:* Kenneth Irons Action Figure    *size:* 6"H

**2**

*sculptor:* **CURT CHIARELLI**
*title:* Interstellar Mobster    *medium:* Urethane Resin    *size:* 141/2"H

**3**

*sculptor:* **LAWRENCE NORTHEY**
*designer:* Lawrence Northey    *title:* Midnight (Game Player)
*medium:* Metal & Plastic    *size:* 29"Hx15"W

**4**

*artist:* **JAMES CHRISTENSEN**
*client:* The Greenwich Workshop    *title:* The Scholar    *medium:* Porcelain
*size:* 8"H

**1**

**2**

**3**

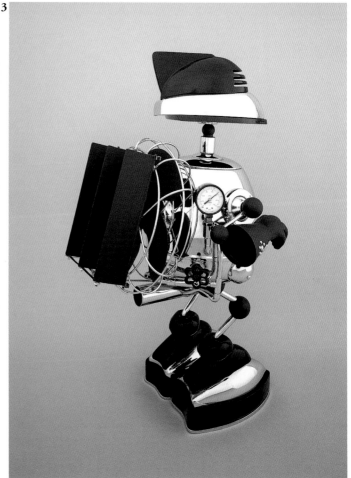

4

1

2

**1**
*sculptor:* **THE SHIFLETT BROS.**
*art director:* Glen Danzig   *designer:* Simon Bisley   *client:* Verotik   *title:* Satanika
*medium:* Soper Sculpey/Resin   *size:* 10"H

**2**
*sculptor:* **BARSOM MANASHIAN**
*art director:* Barsom Manashian   *designer:* Chris Cooper [Coop]   *title:* Devil Girls
*medium:* Cold-Cast Resin   *size:* 12"H

**3**
*sculptor:* **BARSOM MANASHIAN**
*art director:* Barsom Manashian   *designer:* Brom   *title:* Miss Muffit
*medium:* Cold-Cast Resin   *size:* 12"H

3

**1**
*sculptor:* **DENNIS T. KAUTH**
*art director:* Dennis T. Kauth
*designer:* Dennis T. Kauth
*client:* T.S.R., Inc.
*title:* Fraal City Ship
*medium:* Foam, wood & metal
*size:* 36"D

**2**
*sculptor:* **TOM TAGGART**
*art director:* Grendel
*photographer:* Sal Trombino
*client:* Ed Lemco
*title:* Die Blau Engelin
*medium:* Mixed

**3**
*sculptor:* **LAWRENCE NORTHEY**
*designer:* Lawrence Northey
*title:* Chyx & Method
*medium:* Metal & plastic
*size:* 31"Wx36"H

**4**
*sculptor:* **TOM TAGGART**
*art director:* Phil Amara
*photographer:* Sal Trombino
*client:* Dark Horse Comics
*title:* Predator
*medium:* Mixed
*size:* 20"Wx29"H

**5**
*sculptor:* **HARRIETT MORTON BECKER**
*designer:* Harriett Morton Becker
*client:* Private Collection
*title:* Guardian of the Gate
*medium:* Clay
*size:* 19"H

**6**
*sculptor:* **SANDRA LIRA**
*title:* Sentinel
*medium:* Cast Resin
*size:* 43"H

1

2

3

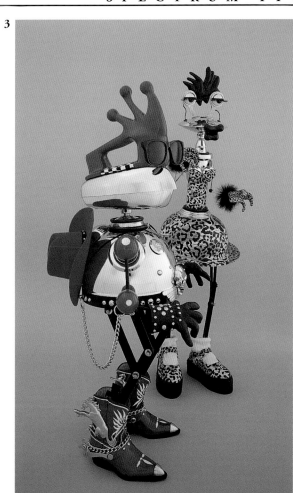

4

5

6

**1**
*sculptor:* **ROBERT CRUMB**
*title:* Devil Girl   *medium:* Painted wood

**2**
*sculptor:* **LISA SNELLINGS**
*art director:* Lisa Snellings   *designer:* Lisa Snellings
*photographer:* Greg Staley
*client:* Howard & Jane Frank
*title:* Short Trip to October   *medium:* Mixed
*size:* 6'Wx41/2'H

**3**
*sculptor:* **JOEL HARLOW**
*title:* Nyarlathotep   *medium:* Bronze   *size:* 18"H

**4**
*sculptor:* **VINCENT CANTILLON**
*title:* Avenging Angel   *medium:* Bronze   *size:* 33"H

1

2

3

4

*artist:* THOM ANG
*designer:* Thom Ang    *client:* Business Week 9/22    *title:* Can We End Heart Disease?    *size:* 71/2"x8"    *medium:* Mixed

*artist:* **JAMES GURNEY**
*art director:* **Chris Sloan**     *client:* **National Geographic**     *title:* **Giganotosaurus**     *size:* **18"x24"**     *medium:* **Oil on board**

**1**
*artist:* **HAJIME SORAYAMA**
*art director:* Eugene Wang    *designer:* Eugene Wang
*client:* Imagine Media    *title:* PlayStation Magazine    *medium:* Mixed    *size:* 8"x10 1/2"

**2**
*artist:* **MATTHEW D. WILSON**
*art director:* Shauna Wolf Narciso    *client:* Duelist/Wizards of the Coast
*title:* Dark Angel    *medium:* Acrylic    *size:* 11"x14"

**3**
*artist:* **R.K.POST**
*art director:* Larry Smith    *client:* Dragon Magazine
*title:* Leave Sleeping Dragons Lie    *medium:* Oil    *size:* 14"x20"

**4**
*artist:* **DiTERLIZZI**
*art director:* Dave Gross    *designer:* Larry Smith    *client:* Dragon Magazine
*title:* A Golden Afternoon    *medium:* Watercolor & gouache    *size:* 20"x30"

**5**
*artist:* **ELIZABETH LAWHEAD BOURNE**
*art director:* Thea Hardy    *designer:* Thea Hardy    *client:* SFWA Bulletin
*title:* Greetings    *medium:* digital

1

2

3

4

5

**1**
*artist:* **MARCO VENTURA**
*art director:* Tom Staebler
*designer:* Kerig Pope
*client:* Playboy Enterprises, Inc.
*title:* The Battle of Khafji

**2**
*artist:* **DONATO GIANCOLA**
*art director:* Tom Staebler
*designer:* Kerig Pope
*client:* Playboy Enterprises, Inc.
*title:* The Wire Continuum

**3**
*artist:* **WILLIAM JOYCE**
*client:* The New Yorker

3

**1**
*artist:* **ARTHUR ADAMS**
*art director:* Eugene Wang   *designer:* Eugene Wang   *client:* Imagine Media   *title:* PlayStation Magazine
*medium:* Pen & ink   *size:* 8"x10 1/2"

**2**
*artist:* **KAREN BARNES**
*art director:* Will Hopkins   *designer:* Beth Lin   *client:* Kids Discover
*title:* Ocean Myths   *medium:* Mixed   *size:* 10"x10"

**3**
*artist:* **KERRY P. TALBOTT**
*art director:* Tom Bond   *client:* Richmond Times-Dispatch
*title:* Hot Head   *medium:* Mixed   *size:* 10"x16"

**4**
*artist:* **WILLIAM STOUT**
*art director:* James Breitbeil
*designer:* William Stout
*client:* Frank Frazetta Fantasy Magazine
*title:* Dinosaur Parade
*medium:* Ink & watercolor
*size:* 8"x12"

1

2

3

4

1

2

**1**
*artist:* **JOSEPH DeVITO**
*art director:* Jonathan Schneider   *client:* Mad Magazine   *title:* Alfred E. Presley
*medium:* Oils   *size:* 18"x25"

Alfred E. Newman ®, ™, and copyright © 1998 by EC Publications, Inc. All Rights Reserved.

**2**
*artist:* **GREG SPALENKA**
*art director:* Tom DeMay   *client:* Internet Underground   *title:* Internet Underground
*medium:* Mixed   *size:* 8"x11"

**3**
*artist:* **MEL ODOM**
*art director:* Tom Staebler   *designer:* Kerig Pope   *client:* Playboy Enterprises, Inc.
*title:* Three Balconies

3

**1**
*artist:* **ISTVAN BANYAI**
*art director:* Tom Staebler
*designer:* Kerig Pope
*client:* Playboy Enterprises, Inc.
*title:* Coed Confidential

**2**
*artist:* **IAN MILLER**
*art director:* Carl Gnam
*client:* Sovereign Media, Inc.
*title:* Lord of the Fiery Depths
*medium:* Acrylic & inks
*size:* 141/2"x111/2"

**3**
*artist:* **IAN MILLER**
*art director:* Carl Gnam
*client:* Sovereign Media, Inc.
*title:* Death on the Reik
*medium:* Acrylic & inks
*size:* 12"x16"

1

2

3

**1**
*artist:* **ALLEN G. DOUGLAS**
*art director:* Steve Blackwell
*client:* InQuest
*title:* Blood of the Phoenix
*medium:* Oil on paper
*size:* 10"x16"

**2**
*artist:* **GEORGE H. KRAUTER**
*art director:* Carl Gnam/
George H. Krauter
*client:* Science Fiction Age
*medium:* Digital

**3**
*artist:* **KEVIN KRENECK**
*art director:* Anthony Bari
*designer:* Anthony Bari
*client:* Alfred Hitchcock's
Mystery Magazine
*title:* The Devil to Pay
*medium:* Pen & ink
*size:* 51/4"x8"

**4**
*artist:* **FRED STONEHOUSE**
*art director:* Tom Staebler
*designer:* Kerig Pope
*client:* Playboy Enterprises, Inc.
*title:* The Slings of Desire

1

2

3

4

*artist:* DAVID DeVRIES

*art director:* David DeVries     *designer:* David DeVries     *client:* Dark's Art Parlour     *title:* These Things'll Kill Ya

*size:* 22"x32"     *medium:* Mixed

**1**
*artist:* **MICHAEL SUTFIN**
*art director:* Jim Nelson
*client:* FASA Corporation
*title:* Elite Security Mage
*medium:* Oils

**2**
*artist:* **ROB ALEXANDER**
*art director:* Matt Wilson
*client:* Legend of the 5 Rings
*title:* Honor's Vale
*medium:* Watercolor   *size:* 10"x13"

**3**
*artist:* **MURRAY TINKELMAN**
*art director:* Joe Glisson
*designer:* Joe Glisson
*client:* Dellas Graphics
*title:* Locomotoad
*medium:* Pen & ink   *size:* 9"x12"

**4**
*artist:* **MICHAEL SUTFIN**
*art director:* Jim Nelson
*client:* FASA Corporation
*title:* Craig Anarchy #1
*medium:* Oils   *size:* 13"x15 1/2"

1

2

3

**1**
*artist:* **JAMES CHRISTENSEN**
*client:* Portal Publications
*title:* Conversation Around A Fish
*medium:* Oils   *size:* 18"x24"

**2**
*artist:* **JAMES CHRISTENSEN**
*client:* Portal Publications
*title:* Quartet
*medium:* Acrylic   *size:* 24"x30"

**3**
*artist:* **SCOTT GUSTAFSON**
*art director:* Jennifer Oakes
*designer:* Scott Gustafson
*client:* The Greenwich Workshop
*title:* The Owl and the Pussycat
*medium:* Oils   *size:* 20"x24"

**1**
*artist:* **DAVID BOWERS**
*client:* Scott Hull Associates   *title:* The Pumpkin's Revenge
*medium:* Oil on masonite   *size:* 12"x12"

**2**
*artist:* **DOUGLAS KLAUBA**
*title:* Angel In Green   *medium:* Acrylic   *size:* 201/4"x261/4"

**3**
*artist:* **RAFAL OLBINSKI**
*client:* Nathan Galleries   *title:* Olbinski Calendar
*medium:* Acrylic

**4**
*artist:* **DAVID BOWERS**
*title:* Dead Butterfly   *medium:* Oil on masonite
*size:* 121/2"x22"

1

2

3

4

**1**
*artist:* **DON MAITZ**
*client:* Lone Star Con 2
*title:* Lone Star 2
*medium:* Acrylic on masonite
*size:* 18"x30"

**2**
*artist:* **JEFFREY K. BEDRICK**
*title:* Asylum  *medium:* Oil
*size:* 30"x40"

**3**
*artist:* **YURI BARTOLI**
*title:* Spaceport
*medium:* Oil on masonite
*size:* 333/4"x433/4"

**4**
*artist:* **JACQUES BREDY**
*art director:* Mike Lund
*client:* Vert-H
*title:* Clone Slayers
*medium:* Oils
*size:* 20"x30"

1

2

3

4

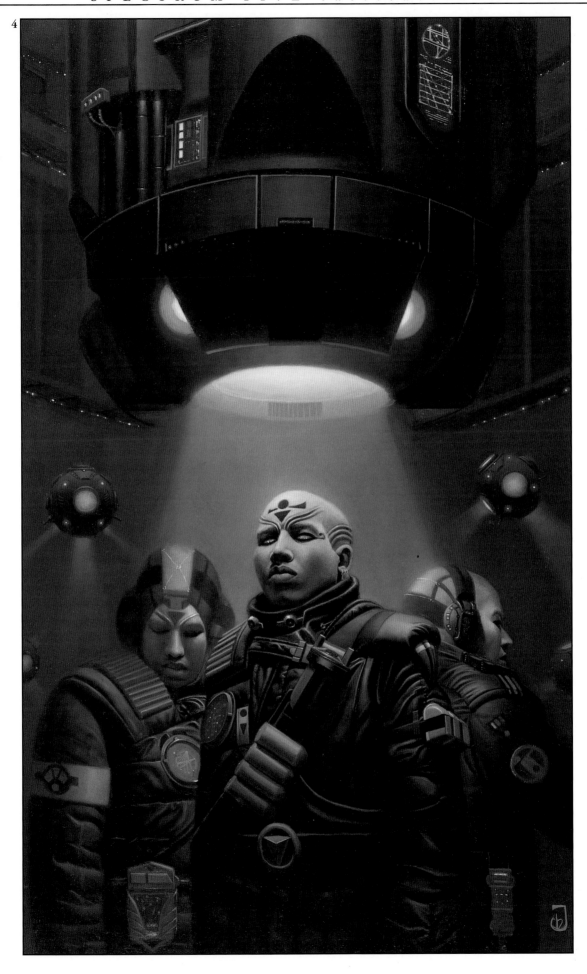

**1**
*artist:* **SCOTT M. FISHER**
*art director:* Sue Ann Harkey
*client:* Wizards of the Coast
*title:* Deep Sea Serpent
*medium:* Acrylic

**2**
*artist:* **SCOTT M. FISHER**
*art director:* Sue Ann Harkey
*client:* Wizards of the Coast
*title:* Minotaur Warrior
*medium:* Acrylic

**3**
*artist:* **ALISTER LOCKHART**
*art director:* Nick Stathopoulos
*client:* Strategic Studies Group
*title:* Promotion
*medium:* Acrylic
*size:* 8"x10"

**4**
*artist:* **BRIAN DESPAIN**
*art director:* Neal Darcy
*client:* Ronin Publishing
*title:* Dark Tattoos
*medium:* Pencil
*size:* 81/2"x11"

**5**
*artist:* **BRIAN DESPAIN**
*art director:* Neal Darcy
*client:* Ronin Publishing
*title:* The Gate Keeper
*medium:* Pencil
*size:* 5"x5"

**6**
*artist:* **WES BENSCOTER**
*client:* SMH/Hobby Japan
*title:* Witch With Tentacles
*medium:* Acrylic
*size:* 18"x24"

1

2

3

4

5

6

**1**
*artist:* **MARK HARRISON**
*art director:* Mark Harrison    *title:* Sara Stockbridge 4    *medium:* Acrylic & gold leaf
*size:* 71/4"x28"

**2**
*artist:* **DiTERLIZZI**
*art director:* Oliver Hoffman    *client:* Feeler & Schwert    *title:* The Changelings
*medium:* Gouache    *size:* 20"x30"

**3**
*artist:* **PETAR MESELVŽIJA**
*art director:* Chris Meiklejohn    *client:* Meiklejohn Graphics    *title:* The Gate Girl
*medium:* Oils    *size:* 50cmx70cm

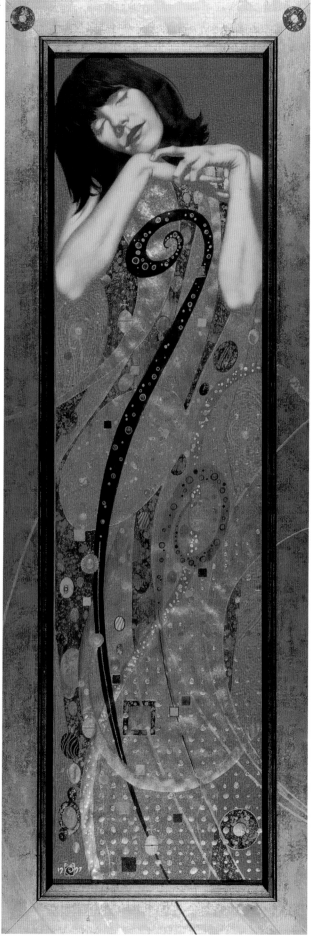

1

2

3

**1**
*artist:* **PHILIP STRAUB**
*art director:* Philip Straub   *title:* In the Middle

**2**
*artist:* **JEFF MIRACOLA**
*title:* Fear of Flying   *medium:* Oils   *size:* 14"x14"

**3**
*artist:* **JOE CHIODO**
*art director:* Sal Quartuccio   *designer:* Joe Chiodo
*client:* S.Q. Productions, Inc.   *title:* Dino Babe
*medium:* Acrylic   *size:* 12"x14"

**4**
*artist:* **JEFF MIRACOLA**
*title:* Gathering of the Mice Men   *medium:* Oils
*ize:* 18"x24"

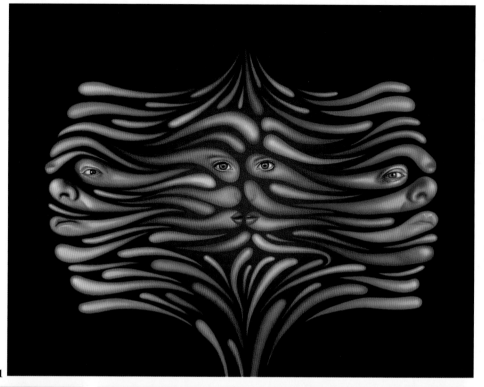

1

2

3

4

**1**
*artist:* **BOB EGGLETON**
*client:* Hamilton
*title:* Tyrant   *medium:* Acrylic   *size:* 12"x12"

**2**
*artist:* **ENI OKEN**
*title:* Bag on Stage
*medium:* 3-D Digital

**3**
*artist:* **WILLIAM STOUT**
*art director:* William Stout
*client:* Sega GameWorks
*title:* Guilty Pleasures
*medium:* Ink & watercolor
*size:* 10"x13"

**4**
*artist:* **SEAN O'KEEFE**
*title:* Landscape With Self
*medium:* Oil
*size:* 24"x18"

**5**
*artist:* **ENI OKEN**
*title:* Zork Grand Inquisitor
Bridge-Spell Press
*medium:* 3-D Digital
Copyright © 1997 Activision, Inc.

**6**
*artist:* **JUDY YORK**
*art director:* Judy York
*title:* Lightsong
*medium:* Digital

**7**
*artist:* **TITO SALOMNI**
*art director:* Louis Schultz
*client:* Milk & Honey
*title:* The Dream Builder
*medium:* Oils   *size:* 3'x4'

1

2

3

4

5

6

7

**1**
*artist:* **MARK COVELL**
*medium:* Oils   *size:* 18"x24"

**2**
*artist:* **TERESE NIELSEN**
*art director:* Dwight Zimmerman   *client:* Topps   *title:* Xena Warrior Princess
*medium:* Mixed

**3**
*artist:* **DAVID DeVRIES**
*art director:* David DeVries   *client:* Dullas Graphics   *title:* Count Frogula
*medium:* Mixed   *size:* 81/2"x11"

**4**
*artist:* **TRAVIS LOUIE**
*title:* Chester's Dream   *medium:* Acrylic & ink   *ize:* 24"x35"

**1**

**2**

**3**

4

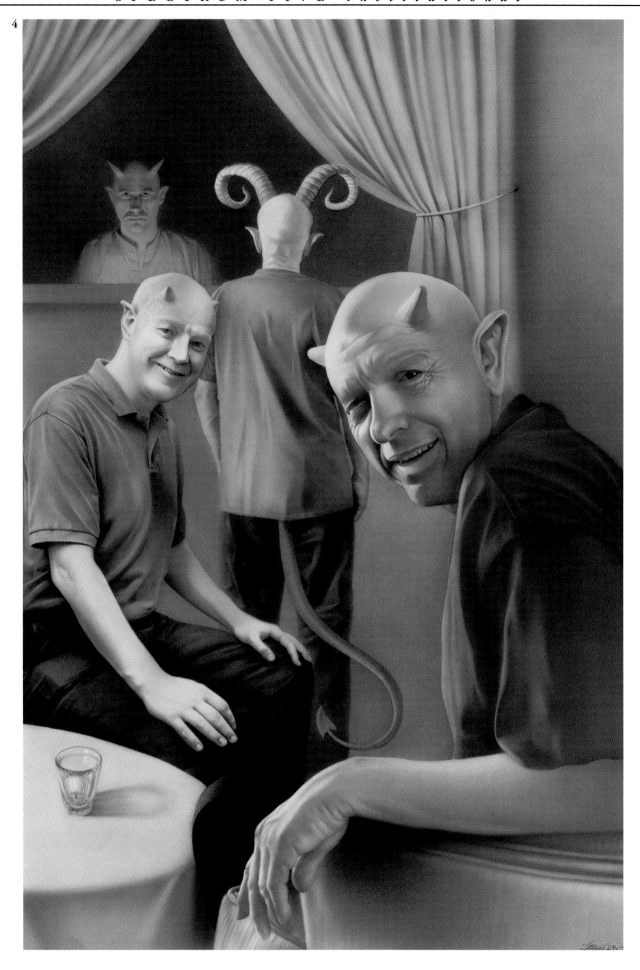

**1**
*artist:* **KIRK REINERT**
*art director:* Kirk Reinert/
Lilli Farrell
*title:* First Light
*medium:* Acrylic    *size:* 22"x33"

**2**
*artist:* **KENT WILLIAMS**
*art director:* Kent Williams
*client:* Allen Spiegel Fine Arts/
4 Color Gallery
*title:* Cradle
*medium:* Watercolor    *size:* 18"x30"

**3**
*artist:* **KENT WILLIAMS**
*art director:* Kent Williams
*client:* Allen Spiegel Fine Arts/
4 Color Gallery
*title:* Cradle
*medium:* Watercolor    *size:* 18"x30"

**4**
*artist:* **KENT WILLIAMS**
*art director:* Kent Williams
*client:* Allen Spiegel Fine Arts/
4 Color Gallery
*title:* KoKoro
*medium:* Mixed    *size:* 18"x30"

4

**1**
*artist:* **DAREN BADER**
*art director:* Matt Wilson
*client:* Wizards of the Coast
*title:* Charging Rhino
*medium:* Acrylic   *size:* 7 1/2"x10"

**2**
*artist:* **JAMES GURNEY**
*art director:* Carl Herrman
*client:* U.S. Postal Service
*title:* The World of Dinosaurs
*medium:* Oils   *size:* 24"x20"

**3**
*artist:* **JERRY LOFARO**
*art director:* Jeff Varsano
*client:* Fun Raisers, U.S.A.
*title:* T-Rex
*medium:* Acrylic   *size:* 13"x18"

**4**
*artist:* **AARON BOYD**
*title:* Tortoise & Hare II
*medium:* Oil   *size:* 30"x40"

**5**
*artist:* **ED LI**
*art director:* Cliff Nielsen   *designer:* Ed Li
*title:* Bully and the Beast
*medium:* Acrylic   *size:* 18"x10"

**1**

**2**

*A scene in Colorado, 150 million years ago*

*A scene in Montana, 75 million years ago*

3

4

5

**1**

*artist:* **THOM ANG**
*art director:* Chris Carter
*client:* 20th Century Fox/Lookout
*title:* Expulsion From Eden   *medium:* Mixed/digital
*size:* 10 1/4"x11"

**2**

*artist:* **THOM ANG**
*art director:* John D'Agostino
*designer:* Thom Ang/John D'Agostino
*client:* 20th Century Fox Home Entertainment
*title:* Clyde Bruckman's Final Repose
*medium:* Mixed/digital   *size:* 8"x11"

**3**

*artist:* **THOM ANG**
*art director:* John D'Agostino
*designer:* Thom Ang/John D'Agostino
*client:* 20th Century Fox Home Entertainment
*title:* Paper Clip   *medium:* Mixed/digital   *size:* 8"x11"

**4**

*artist:* **THOM ANG**
*art director:* John D'Agostino
*designer:* Thom Ang/John D'Agostino
*client:* 20th Century Fox Home Entertainment
*title:* 731   *medium:* Mixed/digital   *size:* 8"x11"

**1**

**2**

**3**

4

**1**

*artist:* **PETAR MESELDŽIJA**
*art director:* Aletta Wiersma   *designer:* Petar Meseldžija
*client:* Vererke Licensing & King International
*medium:* Watercolor   *size:* 32.5cmx23.5cm

**2**

*artist:* **SHEILA RAYYAN**
*client:* Mother Spoon Studio   *title:* Catfish
*medium:* Pencil   *size:* 8"x41/2"

**3**

*artist:* **DOUG MILLER**
*title:* Dragon's Lair   *medium:* Acrylic   *size:* 30"x20"

**4**

*artist:* **OMAR RAYYAN**
*art director:* Jason Hawkins   *client:* Iron Crown Enterprises
*title:* Tūma   *medium:* Watercolor   *size:* 91/2"x11"

**5**

*artist:* **RAY-MEL CORNELIUS**
*title:* Answer Me   *medium:* Acrylic   *size:* 9"x9"

**6**

*artist:* **OMAR RAYYAN**
*art director:* Jason Hawkins   *client:* Iron Crown Enterprises
*title:* We Have Come To Kill
*medium:* Watercolor   *size:* 91/2"x11"

**7**

*artist:* **DON MAITZ**
*art director:* Toby Schwartz
*client:* The Science Fiction Book Club
*title:* Fault Lines   *medium:* Oil on masonite   *size:* 18"x24"

**8**

*artist:* **OMAR RAYYAN**
*art director:* Jason Hawkins   *client:* Iron Crown Enterprises
*title:* Orcs of Udûn   *medium:* Watercolor   *size:* 91/2"x11"

**1**

**2**

**3**

4

5

6

7

8

**1**

*artist:* **KENT WILLIAMS**
*art director:* Kent Williams    *designer:* Kent Williams
*client:* Allen Spiegel Fine Arts/4 Color Gallery    *title:* Communion 2
*medium:* Mixed    *size:* 18"x28"

**2**

*artist:* **JEFFREY JONES**
*client:* FPG    *title:* Back To the Stone Age    *medium:* Oils

**3**

*artist:* **THOM ANG**
*art director:* John D'Agostino    *designer:* Thom Ang/John D'Agostino
*client:* 20th Century Fox Home Entertainment    *title:* Humbug
*medium:* Mixed/digital    *size:* 11"x17"

**4**

*artist:* **GREG SPALENKA**
*art director:* Anthony Padilla    *designer:* Jeff Burne/Greg Spalenka
*client:* Art Institute of Sothern California    *title:* Reborn
*medium:* Mixed/digital    *size:* 18"x24"

**1**

**2**

**3**

4

**1**
*artist:* **LUIS ROYO**
*art director:* Luis Royo   *client:* Norma Editorial   *title:* Millennium
*medium:* Acrylic   *size:* 18"x24"

**2**
*artist:* **DAVID HO**
*client:* American Showcase   *title:* Voices In My Head   *medium:* Digital

**3**
*artist:* **JOHN ZELEZNIK**
*client:* Michael McKnight   *medium:* Acrylic   *size:* 39"x19"

**4**
*artist:* **RAFAL OLBINSKI**
*client:* Naman Galleries   *title:* Olbinski Calendar   *medium:* Acrylic

**5**
*artist:* **JOSEPH DeVITO**
*art director:* George Brewer   *designer:* Jim Balent
*client:* DC Comics   *title:* Catwoman   *medium:* Oils   *size:* 30"x20"
Catwoman ™ and copyright © 1998 by DC Comics. All Rights Reserved.

4

5

**1**
*artist:* **DAVID HO**
*art director:* David Ho   *title:* Garden Of Smokely Delights
*medium:* Mixed/digital   *size:* 6"x9"

**2**
*artist:* **WILLIAM STOUT**
*art director:* William Stout   *designer:* William Stout   *client:* Terra Nova Press
*title:* Peace '97   *medium:* Ink & watercolor   *size:* 121/2"x171/2"

**3**
*artist:* **JOE CHIODO**
*art director:* Ted Adams   *designer:* Tobias Queck   *client:* WildStorm Productions
*title:* The Mechanic   *medium:* Acrylic   *size:* 11"x17"

**4**
*artist:* **DANIEL R. HORNE**
*art director:* Daniel R. Horne   *title:* Still Unlucky   *medium:* Oils on canvas
*size:* 30"x20"

**1**
*artist:* **ZOLTAN BOROS & GABOR SZIKSZAI**

**2**
*artist:* **SIEGBERT MEISSNER**

**3**
*artist:* **CARL LUNDGREN**
*art director:* Carl Lundgren   *client:* Gator Press
*title:* Elvis Has Left the Building   *medium:* Oils   *size:* 28"x16"

**4**
*artist:* **BROM**
*art director:* Brom   *designer:* Brom   *client:* FPG
*title:* Seeker   *medium:* Oils

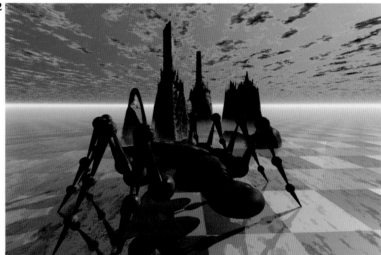

4

**1**

*artist:* **KIRK REINERT**
*art director:* Kirk Reinert   *designer:* Kirk Reinert
*title:* Rising to Greet the Dawn
*medium:* Acrylic   *size:* 45"x35"

**2**

*artist:* **TERESE NIELSEN**
*art director:* Dwight Zimmerman
*title:* Xena   *medium:* Mixed

**3**

*artist:* **BROM**
*art director:* Brom   *designer:* Brom
*client:* Sirius Entertainment
*title:* Moon Blade   *medium:* Oils

**4**

*artist:* **JOE CHIODO**
*art director:* Ted Adams   *designer:* Tobias Queck
*client:* WildStorm Productions
*title:* Freefall   *medium:* Acrylic   *size:* 9"x12"

**1**

**2**

**3**

4

*artist:* **PHIL HALE**
*title:* **Kareoke**    *size:* **20"x26"**    *medium:* **Oils on board**

**1**
*artist:* **MARC FISHMAN**
*title:* Taurus
*medium:* Oil   *size:* 32"x22"

**2**
*artist:* **CHARLES KEEGAN**
*title:* Vengeance In Ice
*medium:* Oil on canvas
*size:* 28"x36"

**3**
*artist:* **CHARLES KEEGAN**
*title:* To the Lair
*medium:* Oil on canvas
*size:* 16"x20"

**4**
*artist:* **MELISSA FERREIRA**
*art director:* David L Porter
*title:* Derring Doer (Page One)
*medium:* Acrylic
*size:* 12"x16"

4

**1**
*artist:* **RICHARD SARDINHA**
*title:* Young Albertosaurus
*medium:* Oil    *size:* 27"x13"

**2**
*artist:* **JAMES NELSON**
*art director:* Matt Wilson
*client:* Wizards of the Coast
*title:* Foul Imp
*medium:* Acrylic    *size:* 9"x6"

**3**
*artist:* **SEAN COONS**
*title:* Dead Dog #7
*medium:* Oil on canvas
*size:* 16"x13"

**4**
*artist:* **MIKE SOSNOWSKI**
*title:* Death Breath    *medium:* Oils    *size:* 20"x30"

**5**
*artist:* **BROM**
*title:* Soulless    *medium:* Oils

**6**
*artist:* **STEPHAN MARTINIERE**
*title:* Alien    *medium:* Digital

**7**
*artist:* **STEPHAN MARTINIERE**
*title:* Demon    *medium:* Digital

4

5

6

7

**1**
*artist:* **MARK HARRISON**
*client:* Phoenix Gallery
*title:* Sara Stockbridge
*medium:* Acrylic & gold leaf
*size:* 18"x25 1/2"

**2**
*artist:* **DANIEL R. HORNE**
*title:* Sea of Tears
*medium:* Oil on canvas
*size:* 40"x30"

**3**
*artist:* **CHARLES KEEGAN**
*title:* Wildcat
*medium:* Oil on canvas
*size:* 20"x30"

1

2

3

1

*artist:* **WILLIAM CARMAN**
*title:* Bait
*medium:* Mixed on ceramic
*size:* 5"x4"

2

*artist:* **MICHAEL DAVID WARD**
*title:* Planet Robot—The Oracle
*medium:* Acrylic
*size:* 15"x20"

3

*artist:* **SHANE JOHNSON**
*title:* Akua
*medium:* Acrylic
*size:* 93/4"x161/2"

4

*artist:* **JOHN JUDE PALENCAR**
*medium:* Acrylic
*size:* 38"x37"

5

*artist:* **JOHN JUDE PALENCAR**
*title:* Between Thoughts of Faith
*medium:* Acrylic
*size:* 57"Wx30"&27"H

1

2

3

**1**
*artist:* **JEFFREY JONES**
*medium:* Oils

**2**
*artist:* **JEFF SADOWSKI**
*title:* Five Fish
*medium:* Acrylic
*size:* 54"x27"

**3**
*artist:* **YURI BARTOLI**
*title:* Durik's Column
*medium:* Oil on board
*size:* 28"x10"

**4**
*artist:* **YURI BARTOLI**
*title:* Merlin Imprisoned
*medium:* Oil on board
*size:* 131/2"x191/2"

4

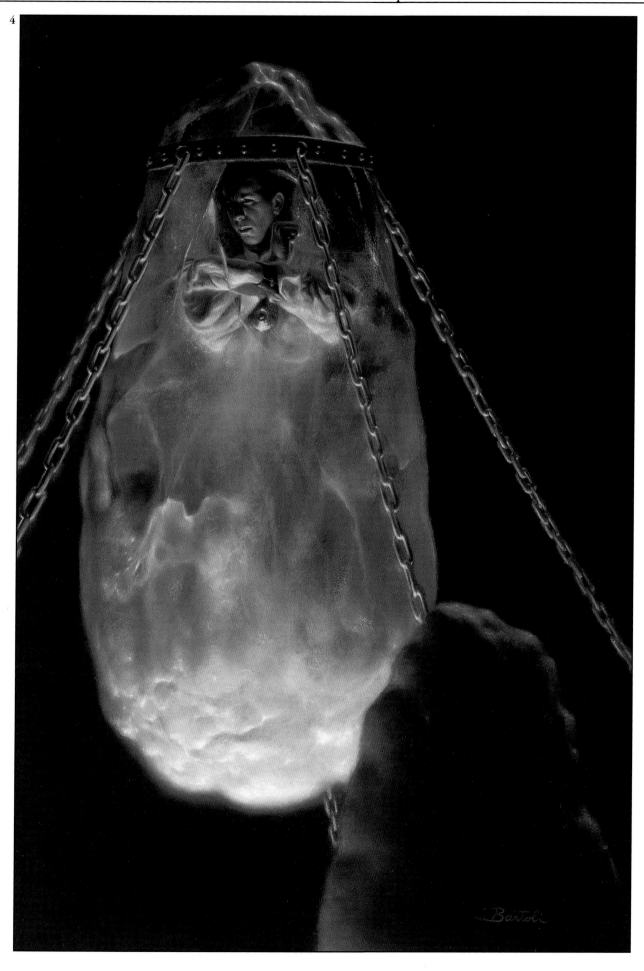

**1**
*artist:* **RAY-MEL CORNELIUS**
*Client:* Mexic-Arte Museum
*title:* Our Lady of Catalina
*medium:* Acrylic on tin  *size:* 8"x10"

**2**
*artist:* **LARRY REINHART**
*art director:* Seven Reinhart
*title:* Engulfed In the Times
*medium:* Mixed  *size:* 11"x16"

**3**
*artist:* **MICHAEL EVANS**
*title:* Early Powers
*medium:* Oil on board
*size:* 20"x30"

**4**
*artist:* **CHRISTOPHER AJA**
*title:* Pumpkin Patch
*medium:* Acrylic  *size:* 7"x13"

**5**
*artist:* **ROBH RUPPEL**
*designer:* Dawn Murin
*client:* T.S.R., Inc.
*title:* Nightmare Lands
*medium:* Oils  *size:* 20"x30"

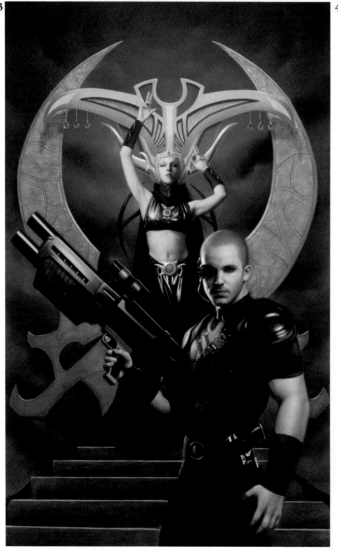

5

**1**
*artist:* **JENNIFER EMMETT WEYLAND**
*title:* Perrin, Queen of Autumn
*medium:* Oils    *size:* 29 1/2"x28 1/2"

**2**
*artist:* **BRIGID MARLIN**
*title:* The Rape of the Earth
*medium:* Oil & egg tempera    *size:* 30"x40"

**3**
*artist:* **ANITA SMITH**
*title:* About To Begin
*medium:* Oil & acrylic
*size:* 18"x24"

**4**
*artist:* **RICHARD HESCOX**
*title:* Poseidon's Daughter
*medium:* Oils    *size:* 11"x12"

1

2

3

**1**
*artist:* **DARREL ANDERSON**
*title:* Crystal Ball
*medium:* Digital    *size:* 10"x10"

**2**
*artist:* **DARREL ANDERSON**
*title:* Filbert Twig Beetle
*medium:* Mixed/digital    *size:* 7"x5"

**3**
*artist:* **CHRISTOPHER LUCIDO**
*title:* Show of Hands
*medium:* Mixed    *size:* 16"x9"

**4**
*artist:* **THOMAS FLEMING**
*medium:* Mixed    *size:* 15"x20"

**5**
*artist:* **JOHN CROCKETT**

**6**
*artist:* **FRANÇOIS ESCALMEL**
*title:* Twilight of the Gods
*medium:* Digital    *size:* 7"x9 1/2"

**7**
*artist:* **MIKE LEHMAN**
*medium:* Mixed    *size:* 18"x18"

1

2

3

4
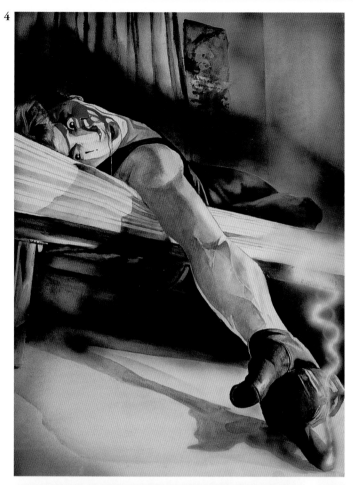

5

6

7

**1**
*artist:* **ILENE MEYER**
*title:* Meyerworld Composite
*medium:* Oils  *size:* 36"x44"

**2**
*artist:* **JEAN-PIERRE NORMAND**
*title:* Titanic's Disaster
*medium:* Acrylic  *size:* 11"x17"

**3**
*artist:* **LEAH PALMER PREISS**
*title:* Fever Dreams
*medium:* Acrylic  *size:* 6"x8"

3

# FEVER DREAMS

**1**
*artist:* **DAVE DeVRIES**
*title:* Turbo Bonnet & Cake Mix
*medium:* Mixed   *size:* 7"x151/4"

**2**
*artist:* **STU SUCHIT**
*title:* Artificial Intelligence
*medium:* Mixed

**3**
*artist:* **MIKE MAUNG**
*title:* Mother   *medium:* Mixed
*size:* 8"x10"

**4**
*artist:* **PHIL HALE**

**6**
*artist:* **RICK BERRY**
*title:* Joey's Room
*medium:* Mixed

**5**
*artist:* **RICK BERRY**
*title:* Islington   *medium:* Mixed

4

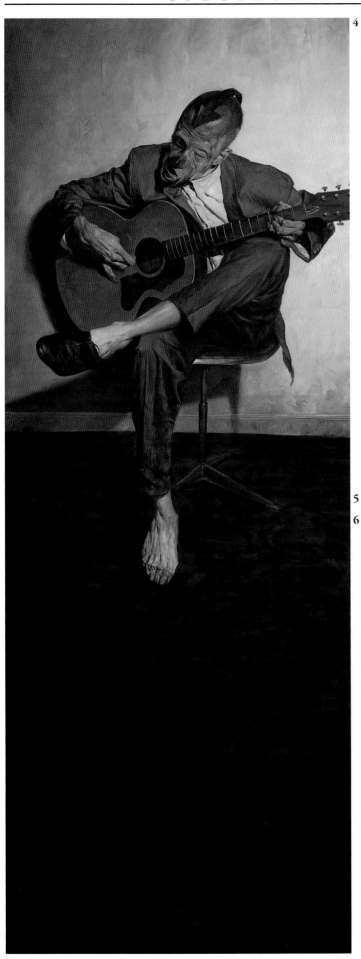

5

6

**1**
*artist:* **PETAR MESELDŽIJA**
*art director:* Miriam de Bondt
*client:* Verkerke Reprodukties
*title:* Snow White and the 7 Dwarfs
*medium:* Oils   *size:* 23cmx40cm

**2**
*artist:* **PETAR MESELDŽIJA**
*art director:* Miriam de Bondt
*client:* Verkerke Reprodukties
*title:* Snow White and the 7 Dwarfs
*medium:* Oils   *size:* 23cmx40cm

**3**
*artist:* **JOHN RUSH**
*client:* The Eleanor Ettinger Gallery
*title:* Study of a Winged Figure
*medium:* Oil on canvas
*size:* 18"x12"

**4**
*artist:* **BRIGID MARLIN**
*title:* Alchemical Days of the Week:
Monday—The Moon
*medium:* Mixed   *size:* 30"x45"

4

**1**
*artist:* **STU SUCHIT**
*art director:* Kay Marshall
*client:* Mix Magazine   *title:* Songs in the Key of Life
*medium:* Mixed

**2**
*artist:* **MICHAEL WHELAN**
*title:* The Wayfarer and the Evening Star
*medium:* Acrylics on canvas   *size:* 36"x24"

**3**
*artist:* **DAVID SEELEY**
*title:* Lost In Thought   *medium:* Mixed

**4**
*artist:* **ROB JOHNSON**
*title:* Alien Jail
*medium:* Acrylic   *size:* 11"x8½"

**5**
*artist:* **MICHAEL ASTRACHAN**
*medium:* Oils   *size:* 20"x28"

4

1

*artist:* **MATTHEW D. INNIS**
*title:* Kinslayer   *medium:* Oils   *size:* 6 1/2"x7 1/2"

2

*artist:* **MARC FISHMAN**
*title:* Virgo   *medium:* Oils   *size:* 20"x40"

3

*artist:* **ATTILA BOROS**
*title:* Song For a Dragon   *medium:* Acrylic   *size:* 15"x23"

4

*artist:* **MATT STAWICKI**
*title:* Dragon's Lair
*medium:* Oils   *size:* 30"x22"

5

*artist:* **STEPHEN HICKMAN**
*title:* The Astonomer Prince   *medium:* Oils   *size:* 48"x26"

1

2

3

4

5

**1**
*artist:* **RICHARD HESCOX**
*title:* Throne of Gold    *medium:* Oils    *size:* 20"x24"

**2**
*artist:* **D. ALEXANDER GREGORY**
*title:* I Am    *medium:* Mixed    *size:* 121/2"x23"

**3**
*artist:* **PAOLO PARENTE**
*art director:* Rafa Martinez    *client:* Norma Editorial
*title:* Martha Demon Hunter    *medium:* Acrylic    *size:* 12"x17"

**4**
*artist:* **STEPHEN HICKMAN**
*client:* Melissa Tripp    *title:* The World's Desire
*medium:* Oils    *size:* 16"x22"

**2**

1

3

4

**1**
*artist:* **JERRY LoFARO**
*title:* Twilight    *medium:* Acrylic    *size:* 11"x14"

**2**
*artist:* **DAVID SEELEY**
*title:* Combat 2010AD    *medium:* Digital

**3**
*artist:* **JON SULLIVAN**
*title:* Spirit of Darkness    *medium:* Oils    *size:* 161/2"x151/2"

**4**
*artist:* **MARC GABBANA**
*title:* The Fright Forwarders    *medium:* Acrylic    *size:* 14"x18"

4

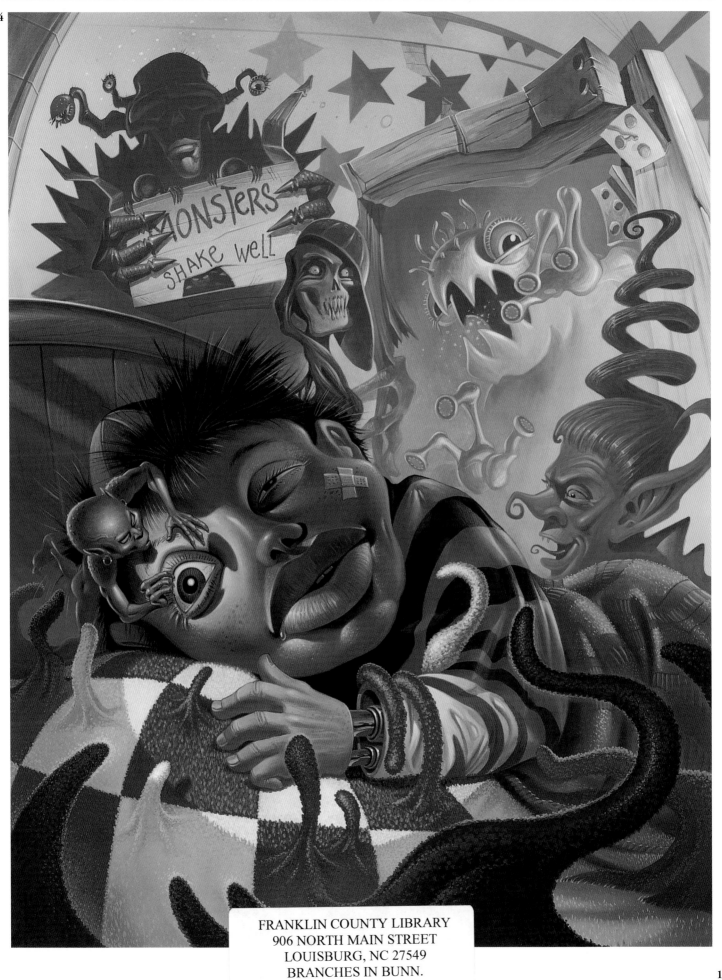

Arthur Adams 88
c/o John Fanucchi
4358 Conejo Dr
Danville CA 94506
adbm3@pacbell.net

Christopher Aja 146

Rob alexander 98
www.robalexander.com

Darrel Anderson 150
www.braid.com

Thom Ang 82, 120, 121, 124
c/o Allen Spiegel Fine Arts
221 Lobos Ave.
Pacific Grove, CA 93950
831-372-4672
asfa@redshift.com

Patrick Arrasmith 9
www.patrickarrasmith.com

Michael Astrachan 159

Daren Bader 118
625 Poinsettia Park N
Encinitas, CA 92024
www.darenbader.com
darenbader.blogspot.com

Istvan Banyai 92
www.istvanbanyai.com

Karen Barnes 89
c/o Woods Ronsaville Harlin, Inc.
www.wrh-illustration.com

Yuri Bartoli 104, 144, 145

Jill Bauman 28
162-19 65th Ave.
Fresh Meadows, NY 11365
www.jillbauman.com

Thomas Baxa 44
www.baxaart.com

Jeffrey Bedrick 104
jeffreykbedrick.com

Doug Beekman 53
doug_beekman@hotmail.com

Wes Benscoter 107
www.wesbenscoter.com

Richard Bernal 11, 40
www.bernalstudio.com

Rick Berry 13, 155
93 Warren St,
Arlington, MA 02174
781-648-6375
www.braid.com

Richard Bober 44
www.wow-art.com

Attilia Boros 130, 160

Elizabeth Lawhead Bourne 85

David Bowers 102, 103
www.dmbowers.com

Aaron Boyd 119
www.aaronboydarts.com

Jacques Bredy 105
www.sym7.com

Brom 62, 131, 132, 139
www.bromart.com

Charles Burns 48
www.charlesburns.com

Jim Burns 18, 26
represented by Alan Lynch
116 Kelvin Place
Ithaca, NY 14850
607-257-0330
alartists@aol.com

Ciruelo Cabral 20
PO Box 57
08870 Sitges
SPAIN
ciruelo@dac-editions.com

Clyde Caldwell 38
www.clydecaldwell.com

Vincent Cantillon 81
www.myspace.com/4889636

William Carman 142
4230 E Trekker Rim Dr
Boise, ID 83716
bcarman@boisestate.edu
billcarman.blogspot.com

Paul Chadwick 56, 57
www.paulchadwick.net

Travis Charest 46, 52, 66
www.travischarest.com

Curt Chiarelli 74
www.thesculptorscorner.com/Chiarelli.htm

Joe Chiodo 110, 128, 133
www.joechiodo.com

James C. Christensen 70, 75, 100
www.greenwichworkshop.com

Sean Coons 138
www.robertseancoons.com

Ray-Mel Cornelius 123, 146
1526 Elmwood Blvd.
Dallas, TX 75224
214-946-9405
rmbc@earthlink.net

Mark Covell 114
www.markcovell.com

Mark Crilley 58
www.markcrilley.com

John Cockett 151

Robert Crumb 40, 80
www.crumbproducts.com

Michael Dashow 28
www.michaeldashow.com

Brian Despain 107
12207 105th Ave NE
Kirkland, WA 98034
brian@despainart.com
www.despainart.com

Joseph DeVito 42, 70, 90, 127
215-822-3002
jdevito4@earthlink.net

Dave DeVries 6, 97, 114, 154
www.themonsterengine.com

Tony DiTerlizzi 15, 85, 108
www.diterlizzi.com

Allen G. Douglas 92
www.allendouglasstudio.com

Les Edwards 14, 31
www.lesedwards.com

Bob Eggleton 17, 36, 112
401-738-6281
zillabob@ids.net

Tristan A. Elwell 36
c/o Shannon Associates
630 9th Avenue
New York, NY 10036
212-333-2551
www.shannonassociates.com

Mark Elliott 45
markelliott.artroof.com

Steve Ellis 55
www.hypersteve.com

François Escalmel 151
www.francoisescalmel.com

Mike Evans 81, 146

Vincent Evans 47, 50
vinceevansart.com

Melissa Ferreira 137
www.melissaferreira.net
buzzworker@cox.net

Steve Firchow 55, 60, 65
www.stevefirchow.com

Scott M. Fischer 106
344 Stebbins St
Belchertown, MA 01007
413-323-0902
www.fischart.com

Mark Fishman 136, 160
www.marcfishman.com
marcfishman@sbcglobal.net

Thomas Fleming 151
www.flemart.com

Jon Foster 41
118 Everett Ave.
Providence, RI 02906
401-277-0880
www.jonfoster.com

Marc Gabbana 4, 8, 165
www.marcgabbana.com

Donato Giancola cover, 42, 43, 86
397 Pacific St.
Brooklyn, NY 11217
718-797-2438
www.donatoart.com

Gary Gianni 26, 27
www.garygianni.com

D. Alexander Gregory 38, 162
www.ainokostudios.com

James Gurney 83, 118
P.O. Box 693
Rhinebeck, NY 12572
845-876-7746
www.dinotopia.com

Scott Gustafson 70, 72, 101
773-725-8338
gustafsn@enteract.com

Phil Hale 18, 134, 155
www.mockingbirdsrelaxeder.com
www.allenspiegelfinearts.com/hale.html

Greg Harlin 37
c/o Woods Ransaville Harlin, Inc.
-410-266-6550
wrh.inc@verizon.net

Joel Harlow 80
www.harlowfx.net

John Harris 16
c/o Alan Lynch Artists
116 Kelvin Pl
Ithaca, NY 14850
alan@alanlynchartists.com
www.alanlynchartists.com

Mark Harrison 108, 140
www.fsartists.com

Richard Hescox 149, 162
www.richardhescox.com

Stephen Hickman 161, 163
845-758-3930
shickman@stephenhickman.com

David Ho 126, 128
3586 Dickenson Common
Fremont, CA 94538
510-656-2468
ho@davidho.com

Daniel Horne 36, 129, 140
www.danielhorne.com

John Howe 34
represented by Alan Lynch
116 Kelvin Place
Ithaca, NY 14850
607-257-0330
alartists@aol.com

Adam Hughes 64
www.justsayah.com

Matthew D. Innis 160
www.innisfineart.com

Nicholas Jainschigg 25
401-245-2954
nickej@earthlink.net

Bruce Jensen 12, 19, 32
718-937-1887
www.brucejensen.com

Rob Johnson 158
www.silverbackworks.com

Shane Johnson 142
www.sljillustration.com

Jeffrey Jones 96, 124, 144

William Joyce 20, 42, 87
www.williamjoyce.com

Joe Jusko 50, 54
www.joejusko.com

Dennis T. Kauth 78

Charles Keegan 34, 136, 141
www.keeganprints.com

Miran Kim 60
www.boyinthewater.com

Douglas Klauba 102
708-229-2507
www.douglasklauba.com

Gyorgy Korga 30

George Krauter 92
gkrauter@G-3D.com
www.G-3D.com

Kevin Kreneck 92
kkreneck@aol.com

Jim Lee 48
www.myspace.com/jimlee00

Mike Lehman 151
www.number36.com

Ed Li 110

Joseph Michael Linsner 50, 63
www.linsner.com

Sandra Lira 79
www.sculptor.net

Alister Lockhart 107
www.alisterlockhart.com

Jerry Lofaro 119, 164
www.jerrylofaro.com

Todd Lockwood 40
20825 SR 410 E #186
Bonney Lake, WA 98390
www.toddlockwood.com

Greg Loudon 51
www.desolateangels.net

Travis Louie 115
www.travislouie.com

Christopher Lucido 150

Carl Lundgren 130
800-795-9272
www.carllundgren.com

Don Maitz 14, 104, 123
941-927-7206
donmaitz@paravia.com

Alexander Maleev 48
www.maleev.com

Barsom Manashian 76, 77

Gregory Manchess 22, 39
www.manchess.com

Brigid Marlin 148, 157
www.brigidmarlin.com

Stephan Martiniere 139
www.martiniere.com

Mike Maung 154
www.allaroundpainters.com

Dave McKean 10, 18
www.asfa.biz
www.davemckean.com

Siegbert Meissner 130

Petar Meseldzija 109, 122, 136
www.petarmeseldzijaart.com
petarmeseldzija@planet.nl

Ilene Meyer 152

Ken Meyer Jr 6
www.kenmeyerjr.com
kenmeyerjr@comcast.net

Doug Miller 122

Ian Miller 92, 93
represented by Jane Frank
www.wow-art.com

Jeff Miracola 110, 111
www.jeffmiracola.com
jeff@jeffmiracola.com

Christopher Moeller 49, 52, 58
www.moellerillustrations.com

Chris Moore 12, 24
represented by Jane Frank
www.wow-art.com
www.chrismooreillustration.co.uk

Clayburn Moore 74
www.csmorestudio.com

Harriett Morton-Becker 79

Dean Morrissey 28
www.deanmorrisseystudio.com

John Mueller 58, 61
www.muellerart.com
muellermail@gmail.com

Jon J Muth 60
www.asfa.biz

James Nelson 138
www.theispot.com/artist/jnelson

Mark A. Nelson 21, 22
www.grazingdinosaurpress.com
gdpmark@chorus.net

Greg Newbold 29
www.gregnewbold.com
801-274 2407

Terese Nielsen 114, 132
626-286-5200
hiddenkingdom@earthlink.net

Jean-Pierre Normand 152
www.jeanpierrenormand.com

Lawrence Northey 68, 74, 79
lawrence@robotart.net
www.robotart.homestead.com

Mel Odom 91

Sean O'Keefe 113
www.masterfung.com

Eni Oken 112, 113
www.oken3d.com

Rafal Olbinski 6, 7, 102, 127
212-532-4328
olbinskiart@yahoo.com

Glen Orbik 66
www.orbikart.com
glenandlaurel@earthlink.net

Margaret Organ-Kean 5
www.organ-kean.com

Zeljko Pahek 17
zpahek@gmail.com

John Jude Palencar 16, 32, 33, 143
330-722-1859
www.johnjudepalencar.com

Paolo Parente 54, 162
www.paoloparente.dust-game.com

Mike Pascale/Dean Armstrong 56
www.myspace.com/mikepascale

Omaha Perez 55
www.omahaperez.com

J.A. Pippett 72, 73
www.lynnlupettigallery.com

R.K. Post 23, 85
www.rkpost.tripod.com

Leah Palmer Preiss 153
www.leahpalmerpreiss.com

Omar Rayyan 122, 123
www.studiorayyan.com
omar@studiorayyan.com

Sheila Rayyan 122
www.studiorayyan.com
sheila@studiorayyan.com

Kirk Reinert 116, 132, 135
www.kirkreinert.com
rep@htbm.ne

Larry Reinhart 146
c/o Carol Newman & Associates
www.carolenewman.com

Laura Reynolds 72

Romas 14, 24
www.romas.biz

Alex Ross 64
www.alexrossart.com

Luis Royo 126
represented by Alan Lynch
116 Kelvin Place
Ithaca, NY 14850
607-257-0330
alartists@aol.com

Steve Rude 52, 64, 67
www.steverude.com
steverude@steverude.com

Gary Ruddell 32
875 Las Ovejas St.
San Rafael, CA 94903
415-479-1016

Robh Ruppel 8, 44, 147
818-249-9341
ruppel@earthlink.net

John Rush 156
847-869-2078
www.johnrushillustration.com

Jeff Sadowski 144
www.jeffsadowskiart.com

Tito Salomoni 113

Richard Sardinha 138
www.battleduck.com

Mark Sasso 4, 8
www.marcsasso.com
blkmetal1@aol.com

Boban Savic 24, 35
getoart@gmail.com
+38111361912

David Seeley 158, 164
www.daveseeley.com
www.shannonassociates.com

Barclay Shaw 30
www.barclayshaw.com
barclay@barclayshaw.com

The Shiflett Bros. 69, 70, 76
www.shiflettbrothers.com

# SPECTRUM 5 *artist index*

Anita Smith 148

Lisa Snellings 80
www.lisasnellings.com

Hajime Sorayama 84
www.sorayama.net

Mike Sosnowski 139
www.sozstudios.com

Greg Spalenka 2, 56, 90, 125
P.O. Box 884
Woodland Hills, Ca 91365
818-992-5828
www.spalenka.com

Nick Stathopoulos 12
www.geocities.com/nickpaint/
nickart@ozemail.com.au

Matt Stawicki 161
www.mattstawicki.com

Fred Stonehouse 93
fredstonehouseart.com
fred@fredstonehouseart.com

William Stout 89, 113, 128
626-798-6490
wstout@altrionet.com

Philip Straub 110
www.philipstraub.com

Stu Suchit 4, 139, 154, 158
631-219-3518
www.stusuchit.com

Susumu Sugita 72

Jon Sullivan 164
www.jonsullivanart.com
www.jonsullivanart@aol.com

Michael Sutfin 98, 99
www.mikesutfin.com

Tom Taggart 78, 79
www.tomtaggart.com

Kerry P. Talbott 89
www.freewebs.com/kptalbott

Jill Thompson 62
www.jillthompsonart.com

Murray Tinkelman 98
www.tinkelmanstudio.com

Ezra Tucker 3, 4
719-487-0648
ezratucker155@aol.com

Marco Ventura 86
www.venturamarco.com

Ron Walotsky 30

Michael David Ward 142
www.michaeldavidward.com

Jennifer Emmett Weyland 148

Michael Whelan 158
203-792-8089
whelanart@aol.com

Kent Williams 116, 117, 125
www.asfa.biz
www.davemckean.com

Matthew D. Wilson 85
www.mattwilsonart.com

Barry Windsor-Smith 59
www.barrywindsor-smith.com

Janny Wurts 22
www.paravia.com/JannyWurts/

Judy York 113
www.judyyork.com

Paul Youll 17
represented by Alan Lynch
116 Kelvin Place
Ithaca, NY 14850
607-257-0330
alartists@aol.com

Stephen Youll 38
732-985-0086
www.stephenyoull.com

John Zeleznik 17, 126
hunterz5@earthlink.net
www.johnzeleznik.com

The *Spectrum Annual* is the result of a juried competition sponsored by Spectrum Fantastic Art LLC.
Artists, art directors, designers, students, and publishers who would like to receive a Call For Entries poster (which contain complete rules and forms necessary to participate) can send their name and address to:

## SPECTRUM FANTASTIC ART
P.O. Box 4422
Overland Park, KS 66204
official website: **www.spectrumfantasticart.com**

Posters are mailed out in October each year.